1991

W9-DIZ-955

3 0301 00093685 2

THE SAINT AUGUSTINE LECTURE SERIES

Augustinian Institute
Villanova University

Saint Augustine and the Augustinian Tradition

LIBRARY
College of St. Francis
JOLIET, ILLINOIS

EDITOR

Robert P. Russell, O.S.A.

ASSOCIATE EDITORS

Russell J. DeSimone, O.S.A.

Benedict A. Paparella, Ph.D.

Copyright © 1984 by
Villanova University Press
All rights reserved

Library of Congress Catalog Card Number: 84–50962
ISBN 87723-039-0

922.1
A923fe

THE SAINT AUGUSTINE LECTURE 1982

THE CONVERSIONS OF
SAINT AUGUSTINE

LEO C. FERRARI

Dedicated in Loving Gratitude
To the Memory of my Parents:

**Leo Francis Ferrari
(1904–1959)**

and

**Millicent Josephine Müller
(1897–1978)**

quorum meriti credo esse omne quod vivo

140, 531

CONTENTS

INTRODUCTION

"They must needs be men of lofty stature whose shadows lengthen out to remote posterity." Thus wrote William Hazlitt the nineteenth-century British essayist.[1] There are few men of history better suited to this metaphor than saint Augustine, whose life spanned the fourth and fifth centuries of our era. Indeed, so immense and all-pervasive has been his influence on our culture that the eminent Marrou has well observed that we of the twentieth century are not separated from Augustine by sixteen centuries, but rather joined to him by those same sixteen centuries, for they are so saturated through and through with his influence.[2]

Clearly, we cannot know too much about so important a figure whose enduring thought continues to mold our own. Fortunately (or so it seems at first sight), the opportunity to satisfy this desire for such knowledge lies close at hand in the form of Augustine's own autobiography— his immortal *Confessions.*

However, the widespread popular appeal of this work down through the centuries belies its complexity. As a result of this twofold aspect, the *Confessions* appeals to both the learned and the unlearned. Indeed, the thought has occurred to me that what Augustine wrote of the Bible in his *Confessions* can also aptly be said of this work of his—his own autobiography[3] for it too is indeed written in

1. 'The Indian Jugglers.'

2. H.-I. Marrou, *Men of Wisdom; St. Augustine and his Influence through the Ages* (Trans. Patrick Hepburn-Scott), Harper Torchbooks (n.d.), p. 147.

3. *Confessions;* (hereafter: *Conf.*), 6, 5, 8.

such plain language and with such unpretentious style so that it might appeal to all, yet for those who delve deeper it offers endless intellectual challenges. As one who has spent the last fifteen years or so poring over the pages of the *Confessions,* my findings have been few, compared with the problems that have multiplied prodigiously in the course of my work. Nevertheless, I welcome this opportunity to endow the details of my small studies with some semblance of encompassing unity. But towering over it all, there still looms larger than ever, the majestic complexity of Augustine's masterpiece with its unfailing appeal, not only to the heart, but also to the mind of man. The numerous bibliographies on the *Confessions,* even in the present century alone, are monumental evidence to this latter aspect of its appeal.

While the great saint may well be horrified and appalled by all this relentless dissection of the details of his life's story, nevertheless the fact remains that the intimacy of the *Confessions* affords the modern scholar the rare opportunity of bridging some sixteen centuries and of getting very close to this great giant. This in itself is no mean privilege. Yet there is more. By better understanding the man Augustine, one can also better understand his many other works that have come down to us. Therefore, even taken merely as autobiography, the *Confessions* becomes a most precious key to Augustine's other works. James Olney, in his *Metaphors of Self* has well depicted this invaluable function of an author's autobiography:

A man's autobiography is . . . like a magnifying lens, focusing and intensifying that same peculiar creative vitality that informs all the volumes of his collected works; it is the symptomatic key to all else that he did and, naturally, to all that he was.[4]

Important as this realization is, for present purposes there is the added advantage of an interesting corollary implicit in Olney's expressive metaphor. The corollary is that it is possible to see in *both* directions through the above-mentioned magnifying lens. The result is that one can also bring the author's other works to bear upon the lines of his autobiography. Not only does this permit "reading between the lines" as it were, but like the magnifying lens it allows one to focus on previously invisible levels of meaning. The resulting discovery of hidden detail can be most informative.

Coming next to the topic of conversion in Augustine's *Confessions,* inasmuch as this names a profound change in religious belief, and therefore a critical stage in the author's development, it is obviously of prime importance to the autobiographical aspect of the work. Throughout this work, Augustine depicts himself as wandering along the many crooked paths of error until he is finally converted and at last stands upon the one straight path of truth that leads to eternal salvation.[5] According to this metaphor, the term "conversion" must be used in the singular, since there is only one path (namely Christ) that leads to salvation. This is the traditional viewpoint, in

4. James Olney, *Metaphors of Self; The Meaning of Autobiography,* Princeton, 1972, pp. 3–4.

5. Leo C. Ferrari, 'Christus Via in Augustine's *Confessions,'* *Augustinian Studies* 7 (1976) 47–85.

which it does not make sense to speak of more than one conversion in the *Confessions*.

While the Christian scholar may well agree with this, nevertheless there are other episodes in the work which also merit the descriptive title of conversion, at least in a less absolute sense.[6] Inasmuch as conversion describes a radical change in one's religious beliefs, then one would have to concede that this also applies, in some sense, to Augustine's earlier adoption of the religion of the Manichees. Furthermore, inasmuch as philosophy (particularly of the Platonic variety) had a religious aura in Augustine's world, there is yet another prominent episode in the *Confessions* which would merit the title of conversion. This is the memorable Hortensius episode of the third book which resulted in Augustine's conversion to the pursuit of wisdom, or *philosophia*. The present treatise will be concerned with all three episodes of conversion in the *Confessions*.[7] Since these represent three critical stages in the process ultimately constitutive of the final great personality of Augustine, every detail of each of the stages acquires a transcendent significance.

6. See J.-M, Le Blond, *Les conversions de Saint Augustin,* Paris, 1950, pp. 89–90. At this point in his book, the author, having implied that there were many historical conversions, then affirms that there was really only *one* conversion. The plural in the title apparently derives from the many conceptual diversities that the author subsequently finds in the notion of conversion.

7. *Cf.* Pierre Courcelle, *Recherches sur les Confessions de saint Augustin* (hereafter: *Recherches*), Paris, 1968, pp. 49–92 for the first two senses of "conversion."

THE CONVERSIONS OF
SAINT AUGUSTINE

I THE CONVERSION TO 'PHILOSOPHIA'

Some sixty years ago, in 1921, Maria Peters published an article on Augustine's first conversion ("Augustins erste Bekehrung")[8] which implied that he underwent other conversions; or as the above author also allows, several stages in one graduated process of conversion. The subject of Peters' study was the famous Hortensius episode of the third book of the *Confessions*.[9] As Augustine tells us there, it was the chance discovery, at the age of nineteen (while studying rhetoric) of Cicero's book, *Hortensius* that filled him with an incredible yearning for the wisdom of philosophy, or *philosophia*.

Noteworthy about the episode as described in the *Confessions* is that it is but another example in that work of divine intervention occasioned through the reading of books.[10] However, lest it be thought from this common feature that the Hortensius episode is a mere literary fiction, it must be said that, from numerous references to it in other places in Augustine's works, there can be no doubting the factuality of the episode.[11] As will be seen, this external corroboration stands in marked contrast to another

8. Pp. 195–211 in *Harnack-Ehrung: Beiträge zur Kirchengeschichte,* Leipzig, 1921.

9. *Conf.* 3, 4, 7–8.

10. This is the theme of my 'From Pagan Literature to the Pages of Holy Scripture; Augustine's *Confessions* as exemplary Propaedeutic,' pp. 173–182 in *Kerygma und Logos;* (Festschrift für Carl Andersen zum 70. Geburtstag) Göttingen, 1979.

11. *Conf.* 8, 7, 17; *The Happy Life* 1, 4 (also 10); *Answer to Skeptics* 1, 1, 4 and 3, 14, 31; and *Soliloquies* 1, 10, 17.

account of a reading; that from the book of Paul at the climax of the *Confessions.*[12]

What is amazing about the Hortensius episode is that this discovery of one book made such a profound and lasting impression on Augustine. No doubt the fact of being nineteen at the time is a relevant consideration. However, on the other hand, age did not bring disillusionment. Thus, after publishing the *Confessions* in his mid-forties, Augustine continued to refer to the *Hortensius* (if not to the episode associated with it) some half-dozen times, with the last reference coming when he was sixty-seven.[13] Unfortunately, most of the book is lost to us, so that we cannot analyze the source of Augustine's inspiration.[14]

What we do know from the surviving fragments is the very significant fact that the book extolled the superiority of the study of philosophy to that of rhetoric, and therein, I would suggest, lies one source of the enduring impression that it made upon the young Augustine. As Testard has well observed,[15] that vaunted superiority of philosophy

12. *Conf.* 8, 12, 29.

13. *Against Julian the Pelagian* (421) 4, 15, 78. The other, and earlier references are: *Epistola 130* (412) 5, 10; and *On the Trinity* (399-419) 13, 4, 7; 14, 19, 26. For some interesting considerations on Augustine and Cicero's *Hortensius,* see: J. Doignon, 'La problematique cicéronienne du protreptique du *De libero arbitrio* II, 35 de saint Augustin' *Latomus* 40 (1981) 807-817.

14. Some claim that the little we know of the book would not encourage a reaction like Augustine's (J. J. O'Meara, *The Young Augustine; The Growth of Augustine's Mind up to his Conversion,* 1954, p. 57). For an attempted reconstitution of the text, see Michel Ruch, *L'Hortensius de Cicéron; Histoire et reconstitution,* Paris, 1958.

15. Maurice Testard, *Saint Augustin et Cicéron,* Paris, 1958, pp. 25-26.

would therefore have been a source of conflict for the young Augustine, who was then studying rhetoric. For one thing, with the notable exception of Aristotle, there was a long-entrenched antipathy between the two disciplines.[16] I hope to show that in the case of Augustine, this conflict is much more significant than has been appreciated.

As described in the *Confessions,* the discovery of Cicero's *Hortensius* has several interesting ingredients, some of which can be appreciated by means of the following extract:

> This book, in truth, changed my affections, and turned my prayers to Thyself, O Lord, and made me have other hopes and desires. Worthless suddenly became every vain hope to me; and in an incredible warmth of heart, I yearned for an immortality of wisdom, and began now to arise that I might return to Thee.[17]

The last statement, about arising to return to God, is one of many such allusions to the prodigal son which are woven through the *Confessions.*[18] Again, from other accounts of the Hortensius episode in Augustine's earlier works, it is doubtful if the turning of his prayers to God, let alone the awareness of his actual starting to return to Him, would have had the prominence for the Augustine of nineteen that was later imputed to the experience by the

16. M. L. Clarke, *Rhetoric at Rome; A Historical Survey,* 1963, pp. 7–9.

17. *Conf.* 3, 4, 7. (Pilkington translation).

18. Leo C. Ferrari, 'The Theme of the Prodigal Son in Augustine's Confessions,' *Recherches Augustiniennes* 12 (1977) 105–118.

middle-aged bishop. When such elements are excluded from the original experience, there remain two ingredients which seem to be substantiated by accounts in earlier works than the *Confessions*. First, there is the rejection of "worldliness" in the form of vain hopes and desires; secondly there remains the passionate espousal of *philosophia*.

(*i*) The Rejection of Worldliness

Regarding the former of these ingredients, it is noteworthy that this rejection of worldliness is prominent in a second allusion in the *Confessions* to the Hortensius episode; an allusion which occurs just prior to the final events of the famous conversion-scene in the eighth book.[19] As will be seen, this occurrence is not without significance.

Meanwhile, to the modern mind, the rejection of worldliness and the espousal of philosophy might well appear as two separate issues, which could well be dealt with in like fashion. To a person as idealistic as Augustine, especially at the age of nineteen, such a compromise would have been rejected out of hand. Added to which, there was the fact that in Augustine's era, philosophy was not merely a system of intellectual principles; but also very much a way of life which demonstrated the veracity of its principles by their hold over the philosopher's life. Courcelle has given us a timely reminder that in Au-

19. *Conf.* 8, 7, 17.

4

gustine's age, to become a philosopher involved a complete reorientation of one's life of such magnitude that we can scarcely conceive of it today.[20] There was obviously no place for worldliness in the whole-hearted pursuit of wisdom, especially in the case of the young idealistic Augustine.

If the serious espousal of philosophy involved the rejection of worldliness, as it would have done with the young Augustine, then the career which he was then pursuing aimed in the very opposite direction. The whole aim of his studies in rhetoric was worldly fame and influence. There was therefore an incompatibility between the direction in which Augustine's studies in rhetoric were taking him and the direction in which he desired so passionately to move, as a result of the discovery of Cicero's *Hortensius*. It is also noteworthy here that the dilemma would have stemmed from the idealistic Augustine rather than from the Cicero whose book had inspired him. To Cicero, philosophy was one of the important fields of knowledge with which the skilful orator should be acquainted,[21] if he were to speak wisely.

Furthermore, the young Augustine's conflict was no mere academic problem to be solved by appropriate course-changes at the school of rhetoric in Carthage. As a careful reading of certain sections of the first book[22] of the *Confessions* will demonstrate, Augustine's new-found ar-

---

20. *Recherches,* pp. 58–59.
21. Clarke, *op. cit.* pp. 56–57; 75–76.
22. *Conf.* 1, 9, 14ff.

dent love for philosophy was also an inherent betrayal of the career of fame and fortune for which the infant Augustine had been cruelly conditioned from the earliest years.[23] Humiliation was added to physical abuse in order that the young Augustine would one day blossom out into a famous orator:

> Oh my God! What miseries and mockeries did I then experience when obedience to my teachers was set before me as proper to my boyhood, that I might flourish in this world, and distinguish myself in the science of speech, which should bring me honour amongst men, and deceitful riches![24]

On top of all this, there was the fact that his parents could not afford the grandiose plans that they had for their son, whence the year's delay in sending him on to further studies.[25] Obviously, being but poor folk, they had made considerable sacrifices to promote the young Augustine's education, with a view to his gaining both fame and fortune. All this too would he be betraying by allowing himself to be seduced away from his parents' worldly ambitions for him by following his new-found love of *philosophia*.

Realizing the seriousness of Augustine's dilemma disposes of what otherwise appears as in intrusive element right in the midst of his description of the Hortensius

23. Leo C. Ferrari, 'The Boyhood Beatings of Augustine,' *Augustinian Studies* 5 (1974) 1-14.

24. *Conf.* 1, 11, 14.

25. *Conf.* 2, 3, 5.

episode. Immediately after the first description of the event, Augustine makes what seems at first like an irrelevant interjection:

> Not then, to improve my language—which I appeared to be purchasing with my mother's means, in that my nineteenth year, my father having died two years before—not to improve my language did I have recourse to that book.[26]

Hence, added to the previous considerations there were also the crowning details that Augustine's father had died in the process of trying to further his son's education and that that son now seemed to be reduced to living off his mother.[27] Even worse, as we know from other places, he also had a mistress and an illegitimate son.[28] It can be appreciated therefore that if there were ecstasy for Augustine in the discovery of his love for *philosophia,* there was also considerable agony. It was to be several years before this intolerable situation was to be resolved.

Meanwhile, there can be no doubt that the struggle of the older Augustine against the cruel conditioning of his earliest years was supremely arduous; a fact which has not been sufficiently appreciated. Even his health seems to have deteriorated, so that he suffered from a persistent chest ailment which finally gave him a valid excuse for

26. *Conf.* 3, 4, 7.

27. Though of course, the family's friend and patron, Romanianus, was underwriting Augustine's education. (*Answer to the Skeptics* 2, 2, 3.)

28. *Conf.* 4, 2, 2; also 9, 6, 14.

7

abandoning the onerous task of teaching rhetoric.[29] Significantly too, we hear no more of that malady after he lay down that burdening profession which he roundly condemns on more than one occasion.[30] Likewise too, we can also better appreciate his joy and exultation at being finally liberated from what had become an intolerable burden.[31]

These various considerations are supported by bringing some of Augustine's earlier works to bear upon the Hortensius episode, when an ambivalent and even inconsistent attitude towards worldliness is to be found. Perhaps this is best shown in the *Soliloquies,* written in 386, between his conversion and his baptism. In the text Augustine's initial strong rejection of worldliness weakens considerably under the persistent questioning of Reason.[32] Again in the *Soliloquies,* Augustine claims confidently that it is almost fourteen years since he ceased desiring riches[33]; which is inconsistent with the claim of the *Confessions* that in his thirtieth year he was still longing for honours, gains and wedlock.[34] The lure of honours and a woman's charms are also mentioned in the *The Happy Life*[35] of the same period as the *Soliloquies.* Perhaps most revealing of

29. *Answer to the Skeptics* 1, 1, 3; *The Happy Life* 1, 4; *Conf.* 9, 2, 2–4. *Cf.* B. Legewie, 'Die körperliche Konstitution und die Krankheiten Augustins,' pp. 4–21 in *Miscellanea Agostiniana,* vol. II, ed. A. Casamassa, Roma 1930–1931, especially pp. 19–20.

30. Thus, in the *Confessions* alone, are to be found the following condemnations: 1, 16, 25–18, 29; 3, 3, 6; 3, 4, 7; 4, 2, 2; & 6, 6, 9.

31. *Conf.* 9, 4, 7.

32. *Op. cit.* 1, 10 17–19; 1, 14, 25–26.

33. *Op. cit.* 1, 10, 17.

34. *Op. cit.* 6, 6, 9.

all, is that nowhere in Augustine's earlier works is there a decisive rejection of the worldly hopes that he had come to regard as so empty because of the Hortensius episode.

However, during the dozen years after the discovery of that book, there was an intense and protracted conflict between the two Augustines. On the one hand there was the older, maturer Augustine who would reject worldly fame and fortune, and on the other hand there was the younger Augustine who had been cruelly conditioned from earliest years to relentlessly seek after such things. Just how conscious he was of this lengthy conflict is shown by Augustine through the deliberate portrayal of its resolution in the climactic events of the eighth book of the *Confessions*. It is there that the rejection of worldliness is featured repeatedly in a most insistent manner.

Thus, the Hortensius episode is recalled at length, just prior to the final events of the conversion-scene and with deliberate insistence upon the worldly aspect:

> For many of my years (perhaps twelve) had passed away since my nineteenth, when, on the reading of Cicero's *Hortensius,* I was roused to a desire for wisdom; and I was still delaying to reject mere worldly happiness, and to devote myself to search out that whereof not the finding alone, but the bare search ought to have been preferred before the treasures and kingdoms of this world though already found, and before the pleasures of the body, though encompassing me at my will.[36]

35. *Op. cit.* 1, 4.
36. *Conf.* 8, 7, 17.

Yet again, immediately after the dramatic events of the conversion-scene, it is back to this rejection of worldliness that Augustine refers with a persistent deliberateness, when addressing God: "For Thou didst so convert me to Thyself that I sought neither a wife, nor any other of this world's hopes."[37] These various details harmonize well with Russell's conclusion in regard to that aspect of worldliness comprising riches when he says: "Augustine's resolve to abandon riches was serious and sincere but also provisional and conditional, contingent that is, upon the discovery of certitude."[38]

(ii) The Espousal of "Philosophia"

Turning next to the second aspect of the Hortensius episode there is the ardent love of wisdom itself—or *philosophia*, with which that discovery inflamed the young Augustine of nineteen years. He relates how that book set him on fire with a desire to leave all earthly things and to fly back to God: "How ardent was I then, my God, how ardent to fly from earthly things back to Thee!"[39] A little further along in the text this ardent desire is implicitly identified with the love of wisdom: "In Greek the love of

37. *Op. cit.* 8, 12, 30.

38. Robert P. Russell, OSA, 'Cicero's Hortensius and the Problem of Riches in Saint Augustine,' *Augustinian Studies* 7 (1976) 59–68. The conclusion is found on p. 68. *Cf. Conf.* 6, 11, 18.

39. *Conf.* 3, 4, 8. Compare with the passionate reading of the Psalms in *Conf.* 9, 4, 11, where the recurrence of *legebam . . . ardebam . . .* would seem to betray an understandable association with the Hortensius episode.

wisdom is called 'philosophy,' with which that book in-flamed me." (*Ibid.*).

As for the specific nature of that *philosophia* which had so much won the heart of the young Augustine, it was as indefinite as the eclectic nature of Cicero's philosophical tastes. Nevertheless, Augustine goes on to write of the ex-tremely strong effect upon him of the exhortation to philosophy in Cicero's book:

> I was delighted with that exhortation, in so far only as I was thereby stimulated, and enkindled and inflamed to love, seek, obtain, hold and embrace, not this or that sect, but wisdom itself, whatever it were.[40]

In *The Happy Life,* written some dozen years before the previous extract, another description of the discovery is equally non-committal, when Augustine says:

> From the age of nineteen, having read in the school of rhetoric, that book of Cicero's called *Hortensius,* I was inflamed by such a great love of philosophy that I con-sidered devoting myself to it at once.[41]

That Augustine had in mind a theocentric Neopla-tonic philosophy when writing these lines in 386 is abun-

40. *Conf.* 3, 4, 8.

41. *Op. cit.* 1, 4 (schopp translation). On philosophy and Augustine's earlier writings, see Alberto Pincherle, 'Il decennio di preparazione di Sant'Agostino (386–396),' *Ricerche religiose* 6 (1930) 15–38. This is the first of a five-part series on this important period of Augustine's life. The others are to be found in the same periodical for the next four years. As one of the pioneers in the lengthy study of the impor-tant years immediately following Augustine's conversion, Pincherle is also author of the valuable book: *La formazione teologica di S. Agostino* Roma (1947).

dantly clear from the closing pages of *The Happy Life*. However, that would hardly have been the principal message he derived from Cicero's book during the actual experience some dozen years earlier, which for one thing, did nothing to liberate him from a materialism which would have been the beginnings of appreciating such a philosophy. His philosophical ideas had obviously evolved considerably, crystallizing into the Neoplatonism which is so obvious in his early works that he has been accused of having been converted to Neoplatonism, rather than to Catholicism.[42]

Meanwhile, it would appear that from the date of his discovery of Cicero's *Hortensius,* Augustine was inflamed with a strong desire for a *philosophia* whose nebulousness was matched only by his passionate dedication to it. The next important question was what form this yearning would assume. In this regard, it is noteworthy that he was not at that time acquainted with the warning of Paul against philosophizing according to the elements of this world.[43] On the other hand, he seems to have had sufficient religious background to have prevented him from accepting with unqualified approval any philosophy that did not reverence the name of Christ.[44]

---

42. This is the thesis made famous by Alfaric in his *L'évolution intellectuelle de saint Augustin* Paris, 1918, pp. 371ff. In regard to this kind of thinking, Courcelle has pointed out that the implied inconsistency between Greek and Judeo-Christian wisdoms is more of a problem for the moderns than it was for persons of Augustine's milieu. (*Recherches* p. 12).

43. *Conf.* 3, 4, 8. The warning is from *Col.* 2, 8-9.

44. *Ibid.*

12

From the pages of the *Confessions* we know that the young Augustine next made an unsuccessful venture into the Scriptures,[45] and then, as he puts it, he "fell among" the Manichees.[46] Two reasons for this latter involvement concern us here. The first was their common use of the name of Christ.[47] In the light of his previous remarks, this would have probably given their religion a certain appeal to him. The second and more relevant reason was their promise of imparting the truth.[48] To the young Augustine with his freshly aroused ardour for *philosophia,* this must have been very enticing bait indeed. As we shall see later, when we come to dealing with his sojourn among the Manichees, there are ample reasons for regarding his venture into that sect as another stage in his ongoing quest for *philosophia.*

Meanwhile, during the nine years or so that Augustine spent as a Manichee, it appears that that quest continued unremittingly. Thus, he tells us that during that period he read every book on the liberal arts that he could find,[49] many of which must have been concerned with philosophy.

45. *Conf.* 3, 5, 9. *Cf.* Courcelle, *Recherches,* pp. 60–63. Testard thinks it likely that this venture was caused by memories aroused by the reading of the *Hortensius* (*Op. cit.*) pp. 32–39.

46. *Conf.* 3, 6, 10.

47. Julien Ries, 'Jésus-Christ dans la religion de Mani,' *Augustiniana* 14 (1964) 437–454. For examples of the prominence of Christ in the religion of the Manichees, see Psalms 242–276 in *A Manichaean Psalm-Book,* Part II, vol. II, in *Manichaean Manuscripts in the Chester Beatty Collection,* edited by C. R. C. Allberry, Stuttgart, 1938.

48. *Conf.* 3, 6, 10.

49. *Conf.* 4, 16, 30.

Accordingly, when he was scarcely twenty, he read and understood with ease, Aristotle's *The Ten Predicaments.*[50] Again, by the time he was twenty-nine, he was conversant by heart with many of the doctrines of the philosophers.[51] However, through it all, Augustine probably settled for a skepticism deriving from his first contacts with Cicero.[52] Thus, on several occasions, when about to quit the Manichees, he refers to himself as doubting after the manner of the Skeptics.[53] The most definite evidence of all is the book *Answer to Skeptics,* which he wrote soon after his conversion to Catholicism, and for the very good reason that, as he says of the Skeptics: "their arguments used to disquiet me."[54]

We have followed Augustine so far past the Hortensius episode only because his conversion to *philosophia* was begun there, but remained incomplete. True, the *Hortensius* had aroused an intense ardour in him, but as the portrayal in the *Confessions* implies, it lacked a proportionate object. This being so, then it remained merely inchoate, like the longing for faith without a corresponding reality in which to believe. If that merely inchoate ardour be conceded, at least in Augustine's perspective, then

50. *Conf.* 4, 16, 28.

51. *Conf.* 5, 3, 3. For Augustine's knowledge of philosophy in the early days of his conversion, see: C. Andresen, 'Gedanken zum philosophischen Bildungshorizont vor und in Cassiciacum. Contra academ. 2, 6, 14ff.; 3, 17, 37-19, 42,' *Augustinus* 13 (1968) 77-98; as also: E. König, *Augustinus Philosophus. Christlicher Glaube und philosophisches Denken in den Frühschriften Augustins,* München, 1970.

52. Testard, *Op. cit.* pp. 81-97.

53. *Conf.* 5, 10, 19; 5, 14, 25; 6, 11, 18.

54. *Retractions* 1, 1, 1; *Cf. Enchiridion* 7, 20-22.

it cannot be said that the Hortensius episode witnessed his conversion to *philosophia* in the full and complete sense.

According to the account of the *Confessions* it was to be some dozen years after the above episode, with the discovery of the so-called "books of the Platonists" that the conversion to *philosophia* was completed. The event and its consequences are related in a sober fashion in the seventh book of the *Confessions*,[55] where Augustine tells how he obtained those books from a man "inflated with most monstrous pride"[56] and how those books taught him to look for incorporeal truth. We are fortunate in having other and more informal accounts of that discovery. One extract, from the *Answer to Skeptics* of 386, is most valuable in that it testifies to Augustine's persistent yearning for *philosophia* across the years since the Hortensius episode and also closes with a renunciation of worldliness which is very reminiscent of that episode. Writing to his friend, Romanianus, Augustine then testifies:

> We never slackened in our yearning for philosophy and for the mode of life which won favour among us, and we agreed to make no other plans whatever. We were aiming at it steadily but less eagerly. Yet we thought that we were doing enough. Because we were not yet beside the blaze that was to seize upon us at its height, we thought that the flickering flame by which we were being warmed was the greatest possible fire. But behold! as soon as certain plenteous books . . . exhaled sweet Arabian fragrance over us, as soon as they shed a very few tiny drops of most precious perfume on that diminutive flame, they at once enkindled in me such a conflagration that—incredible, Romanianus, truly incredible; and per-

55. *Conf.* 7, 9, 13–15; 7, 11, 13–15; 7, 20, 26.
56. *Conf.* 7, 9, 13.

haps beyond even your belief in me: what more can I say?—I could scarcely believe it of myself. What importance did I then attach to any honour? Was I affected by human pomp? by a craving from empty fame? or, in fine, by the bond and bondage of this mortal life?[57]

In the above extract we have a description which in its passionate ardour seems even to exceed that of the earlier Hortensius episode, as well it might, for if that earlier episode signified the beginning of Augustine's voyage to the port of philosophy, the above passage signifies his arrival.[58] It is also significant that the same *Answer to Skeptics* which contains the above extract, concludes with a lengthy and favourable consideration of the philosophy of Plato and Plotinus.[59]

As to the date of Augustine's discovery of the books of the Platonists and his subsequent liberation from an all-encompassing materialism, if we are guided by the chronology of the *Confessions* then that discovery could not have been before his twenty-ninth year.[60] That too was the year prior to this arrival in Milan where he was to learn from the bishop Ambrose that one should not think of God, or of the human soul in material terms.[61] In addi-

57. *Answer to Skeptics* 2, 2, 5 (Kavanagh translation). A similar description, with more definite identification of the books as the so-called *libri Platonicorum* is found in *The Happy Life* 1, 4, of the same year as the cited extract.

58. *The Happy Life* 1, 1–5.

59. *Op. cit* 3, 9–20.

60. That is the year of his life to which the fifth book of the *Confessions* is devoted (*Conf.* 5, 3, 3) and it was then that he could not conceive of anything that was not material (*Conf.* 5, 10, 19; 5, 14, 25; 7, 1, 1).

61. *The Happy Life* 1, 4.

16

tion, he there came into contact with Ambrose as an authoritative exponent of a newly-emergent christian Neoplatonism.[62] Therefore, liberated at last from the limitations of an all-encompassing materialism, Augustine was also introduced to a philosophy that could take man beyond himself in his quest for a transcendent God. These discoveries soon resulted in both his return to the Catholicism of his infancy, and also in the rejection of the worldly profession of rhetoric. Consequently, after a sea-voyage of some dozen years, which began with the Hortensius episode of his nineteenth year, the persistent Augustine had at last arrived at the long-sought port of *philosophia*.

In summary then,[63] Augustine had renounced the burdensome profession of rhetoric for which he had been brutally groomed from infancy, in favour of the *philosophia* revealed to him by the Hortensius episode. This was a *philosophia* for which he had never ceased yearning, but whose attainment had been delayed some dozen years. Meanwhile, the yearning for that *philosophia* was an important factor in luring him into the heretical sect of the Manichees. Only with the concept of immaterialism provided by the discovery of Neoplatonism was Augustine in a position to reject materialism in general, and Manicheism in particular. After a hazardous journey of some dozen years he had at last arrived in the long-sought port of philosophy. However, there still remained the exploration of the hinterland, but that is a topic for the third chapter of this treatise.

62. Courcelle, *Recherches* pp. 93–138.
63. *Cf. Answer to Skeptics* 1, 1, 3.

17

II THE "TRAP" OF MANICHEISM

Unlike the conversion to *philosophia,* Augustine's espousal of Manicheism is not depicted in glowing terms in the *Confessions,* which is hardly a matter for surprise, when one thinks about it. The nine years, or so,[64] that he had spent in that heretical sect were years of the profoundest regret to him by the time that he came to writing the *Confessions.* Consequently, any ardour that he may have experienced at the time of his entry into Manicheism was expunged by the bitterness of the intervening years. He therefore depicts his entry into that sect more after the manner of an accident, like falling into a trap: "and so I fell among men proudly raving, very carnal, and voluble, in whose mouths were the snares of the devil."[65]

There were of course other contributing reasons for the above-mentioned regret. Manicheism had been founded less than a century previously by Mani the Persian and was therefore a very late arrival on the scene in the Empire that had, as it were, already almost worn itself out by welcoming so many exotic religions. Moreover, it was a deeply dualistic religion that saw all of creation polarized between the two hostile kingdoms—one of Light and the other of Darkness.[66] Consequently, it was radically dif-

64. Courcelle's observation (*Recherches*, p. 78) on Augustine's consistent inconsistency about the "nine years" was the origin of my study: 'Augustine's Nine Years with the Manichees,' *Augustiniana* 25 (1975) 208–215.

65. *Conf.* 3, 6, 10.

66. For an example of Augustine on this dualism see: *Against the Epistle of Manichaeus* 13, 16, 22–32, 35.

18

ferent from the usual forms of polytheistic paganism that had proven so popular in the Empire.[67] Not surprisingly therefore, Manicheism had been the subject of imperial proscription from as early as 297.[68] Moreover, after an initial lull, the official christianizing of the Empire had exacerbated, rather than mitigated, the condition of the Manichees.[69]

Augustine, of course, was not unaffected by these external circumstances, even after his rejection of the cult. Thus, well after his conversion to Catholicism, he was accused, on more than one occasion, of being a crypto-Manichee.[70] In the *Confessions* Augustine revealed the undeniable fact that he had indeed fallen into that detestable heresy, from which, by the grace of God, he had subsequently been saved. In view of these considerations, as has been noted above, it would be futile to look for recollections of any ardour that he might have felt at the time of joining that sect, whence the idea of falling into it, as if into a trap. However, when one examines the text of the *Confessions* it becomes bountifully evident that he was indeed carried into that trap by the ardour of the Horten-

67. Two very readable books on Manicheism are: F. C. Burkitt, *The Religion of the Manichees*, 1925, and Geo Widengren, *Mani and Manichaeism* (trans. Charles Kessler), 1965.

68. Erich-Hans Kaden, 'Die Edikte gegen die Manichäer von Diokletian bis Justinian,' pp. 55–68 in *Festschrift für H. Lewald*, Basel, 1953, especially p. 56.

69. Kaden, *Op. cit.*, pp. 57ff.

70. *Answer to the Letters of Petilian* 3, 16, 19; *Against Cresconius* 3, 80, 92.

sius episode, and therefore under the influence of his yearning for *philosophia*.[71]

Indeed, except for the saving intervention of his examination of the Scriptures, one can all but see the relation of cause and effect between the two conversions; the first to *philosophia* and the second to Manicheism. As Augustine informs us in the *Confessions,* the one thing which restrained him from giving his unqualified approval to Cicero's *Hortensius* was the fact that it lacked the saving name of Christ which he had revered from his infancy.[72] He was therefore seeking a *philosophia* which incorporated the name of Christ. This, he gives as the reason for his unsuccessful venture into the Scriptures, immediately after the recount of the Hortensius episode.[73] At that time however, as a fastidious student of rhetoric, he was repelled by the unpretentious style of the Scriptures. His new-found ardour therefore propelled him further along his path of investigation with the result that he "fell in" with the Manichees, whose mythology did indeed feature the name of Christ.[74]

This sequence of events is clearly implied by the very details of the text in the *Confessions,* where the repetition of the word "therefore" links the two episodes which follow, to the ardour generated by the Hortensius ex-

71. Courcelle, *Recherches*, pp. 60–67, and E. Feldmann, *Der Einfluss des Hortensius und des Manichäismus auf das Denken des jungen Augustinus von 373,* Diss. Münster in Westfalen 1975.

72. *Conf.* 3, 4, 8.

73. *Conf.* 3, 5, 9.

74. Jean de Menasce, 'Augustin Manichéen,' pp. 79–93 in *Freundesgabe für Ernst Robert Curtius*, Bern, 1956, especially pp. 87–92. See also, Julien Ries, *art. cit.*

perience: first there is the unsuccessful investigation of the Scriptures, then next comes the falling in with the Manichees. Accordingly, immediately after the *Hortensius* episode one reads in the text: *"therefore* I resolved to direct my mind to the Holy Scriptures"[75] followed a few lines further along by *"therefore* I fell among men proudly raving . . ."[76]

It would appear then, that the Manichees offered the ardent Augustine an irresistible bait in the form of an exotic *philosophia* for which he was then pining. This account is strengthened by a convenient detail in his *The Profit of Believing,* written in 391/2 and addressed to a friend Honoratus, who had joined the Manichees along with Augustine. In this work, Augustine says of the Manichees:

> And you know, Honoratus, that for no other reason did we fall in with such men than that they kept saying that by pure and simple reason (*mera et simplici ratione*), apart from all formidable authority, they would lead their willing listeners on to God and free them from all error.[77]

The second requirement, namely of a *philosophia* involving the name of Christ, was fulfilled by the use that the Manichees made of the persons of the christian Trinity; attempting to integrate them into their bizarre system of beliefs. As a result, Augustine says to God in the continuation of the text of the *Confessions:*

---

75. *Conf.* 3, 5, 9.
76. *Conf.* 3, 6, 10.
77. *Op. cit.* 1, 2. Meagher translation.

> Therefore I fell among men proudly raving, very carnal
> and voluble, in whose mouths were the snares of the
> devil (*laquei diaboli*) — the birdlime (*viscum*) being
> composed of a mixture of the syllables of Thy name,
> and of our Lord Jesus Christ, and of the Paraclete, the
> Holy Ghost.[78]

In this passage, by the mention of birdlime, Augustine
is referring to the ancient art of catching birds by spreading
a sticky glue, or birdlime, on the branches of trees.[79] This
explanation is neatly corroborated by an interesting passage in the same section of *The Profit of Believing* to which
reference has just been made. After describing how he was
seeking the breasts of Holy Mother Church to slake his
spiritual thirst, the Manichees then deceived him: "and so
they did to us what deceitful bird catchers are wont to do,
who fix lime-smeared branches near water to deceive
thirsty birds."[80]

The choice of the image of thirsty birds (*sitientes aves*)
is also most compatible with Augustine's symbology from
the aspect of thirst, which he uses in a deliberate manner in
regard to the appetite for spiritual things.[81] As to what

78. *Conf.* 3, 6, 10.

79. *Cf. On the Teacher* 10, 32; *The Magnitude of the Soul* 21, 36.
For an actual recipe, see Pliny's *Historia naturalis* 16, 94, 248. An interesting account of the tradition of the symbolism of the birdlime
metaphor is Courcelle's 'La colle et le clou de l'âme dans la tradition néo-
platonicienne et chrétienne (Phédon 82e; 83d),' *Revue belge de philologie
et d'histoire* 36 (1958) 72–95.

80. *Ibid.*

81. By an interesting consistency, this is particularly true of the *Confessions*, where metaphors of thirst acquire an almost complete dom-
inance over those of hunger from the ninth book onwards, which is one of
the conclusions of my 'The Food of Truth in Augustine's Confessions,'
Augustinian Studies 9 (1978) 1–14.

particular aspect of spiritual thirst was involved in that entrapment of Augustine by the Manichees, we are informed further along in the text of the *Confessions* when he says of himself and the Manichees:

> For I was ignorant as to that which really is, and was, as it were, violently moved to give my support to foolish deceivers, when they asked me, 'Whence is evil?'—and, 'Is God limited by a bodily shape, and has He hair and nails?'—and, 'Are they to be esteemed righteous who had many wives at once, and did kill men, and sacrificed living creatures?' At which things I, in my ignorance was much disturbed.[82]

Further valuable evidence on the Manichees' precise manner of proselytizing is found in *The Christian Combat,* written at the same time (397) as the *Confessions.* This account is also of interest in having what seem like autobiographical elements in it. Augustine explains how the Manichees do not approach the prospective convert with their fantastic mythology about the race of Darkness and the race of Light in conflict with one another. Instead, they keep quiet about such things at first lest "they would be laughed to scorn and everyone would run away from them."[83] Their alternate and safer approach is to select chapters of Scriptures which simple people (*simplici homines*) do not understand and use such chapters to raise the question of the source of evil in the world. When such a simple person cannot answer this question, he is won over by them through curiosity. One is reminded of Augustine's frequent assertion that he was led into the

82. *Conf.* 3, 7, 12.
83. *Op. cit.* 4, 4.

heresy of Manicheism by his obsession with the origin of evil.[84] Moreover, his unsuccessful venture into the Scriptures in the third book of the *Confessions,* just before falling in with the Manichees, certainly shows Augustine up at the time as being a simple person who did not understand those Scriptures. Again, there are Augustine's repeated references to his own ignorance in the third book of the *Confessions*[85] when describing his entrapment by the Manichees.

Finally on the subject of how Augustine was trapped by the Manichees, his book *On the Free Choice of the Will* contains an interesting detail. In that part of the book written as early as 388, Augustine has Evodius ask him why man has a spontaneous and unlearned ability to do evil, whereas to do good man must undergo discipline and education. The problem of the origin of evil so formulated, was of enduring interest to the younger Augustine. Furthermore, his reply to Evodius reveals the subtle but sharp distinction that the problem of evil did not *pull* him into Manicheism, but rather *drove* him into that heresy:

> You propose a question which disturbed me exceedingly (*vehementer exercuit*) when I was still a youth, one which wearied me and drove me (*me . . . impulit*) into heresy, and indeed caused my downfall.[86]

84. *On the Free Choice of the Will* 1, 2, 10; *On the Morals of the Manichaeans* 2, 2.

85. *Nesciebam enim . . . prorsus ignorabam . . . (Conf.* 3, 7, 12); *non noveram . . . (Conf.* 3, 7, 13); *haec ego tunc nesciebam et non advertebam . . . (Conf.* 3, 7, 14). *haec ego nesciens . . . (Conf.* 3, 10, 18).

86. *On the Free Choice of the Will* 1, 2, 4 (Benjamin and Hackstaff translation).

Had Augustine used the wording "dragged me" (*me traxit*), or its equivalent, then the source of the movement would have been the Manichees and their baiting him with the problem. On the other hand, the present phrasing of "drove me" (*me . . . impulit*) places the source of the movement in Augustine himself, as the sense of the quoted extract also clearly requires. The conclusion is that the problem of evil had greatly troubled the young Augustine *before* he met the Manichees. One is reminded of the dark and turbulent passions of the second book of the *Confessions;* which passions overwhelmed the Augustine of sixteen during his enforced year of idleness and subsequently seared his memory for life.[87]

(i) "Their god is the belly" (Philippians 3, 19)

We have already seen that Augustine likens himself (and his friends) to thirsty birds who were trapped by the deceitful Manichees. As was noted, a more extensive examination of the *Confessions* will show that this comparison is but one more example of the more general theme of the Food of Truth which is woven through the entire *Confessions.*[88] In fact, a closer examination of Au-

87. Leo C. Ferrari, 'Symbols of Sinfulness in Book II of Augustine's Confessions,' *Augustinian Studies* 2 (1971) 93–104. From this grew another study on the subject of the barren field (published in 1977). To me, the second book is particularly memorable for an interesting interplay of the ideas of vegetation and sin. The most outstanding example is of course the famous pear-theft on which I published a study in 1970. Subsequently, in response to an interesting criticism by Courcelle, I was stimulated to produce a study entitled 'The Arboreal Polarization in Augustine's Confessions' (1979).

88. See above, footnote 81.

LIBRARY
College of St. Francis
JOLIET, ILLINOIS

140, 531

gustine's account of his falling in with the Manichees in *Conf.* 3, 6, 10-11 will show that the passages are particularly rich in what may be termed alimentary allusions. Thus, right at the start, he refers to the Manichees "in whose mouths were the snares of the devil." Then a few lines further along he says of the Manichees' efforts at presenting their doctrines to him: "and these were the dishes on which to me, hungering for Thee, they, instead of Thee, served up the sun and moon." [89]

This metaphor is repeated further along in the text when he relates how he fed upon the myths of the Manichees, without however being nourished by them. He also describes how he continued to hunger and thirst after God and later remarks on the poor nutritional value of food seen in dreams. Considerations pass on to include two allusions to the prodigal son who was reduced to feeding swine after his inheritance was wasted. In the second of these Augustine refers to himself as follows: "far indeed, was I wandering away from Thee, being even shut out from the very husks of the swine, whom with husks I fed." [90]

After this, yet more alimentary allusions lead on to the interesting example of the enigmatical woman of *Proverbs* 9:

> I came upon that bold woman, who 'is simple and knoweth nothing,' the enigma of Solomon, sitting 'at the door of the house on a seat,' and saying, 'stolen waters are sweet, and bread eaten in secret is pleasant.' This woman seduced me, because she found my soul

89. *Conf.* 3, 6, 10; *Cf. Conf.* 5, 3, 3; 5, 6, 10.
90. *Conf.* 3, 6, 11.

beyond its portals, dwelling in the eye of my flesh, and thinking on such food as through it I had devoured.[91]

Here, yet again, there are alimentary allusions, and indeed the last of the lengthy series associated with the introduction of the Manichees into the story of the *Confessions*. However, before dealing with this particular topic, it is instructive to look at several aspects of the example of the enigmatical woman. The idea, that perhaps this represents the woman with whom Augustine lived, has to be discounted because of chronological inconsistency.[92] Another aspect of more fruitful interest is the reference to eating bread in secret. As will be seen, diet, and indeed a selective vegetarian diet, was an important aspect of the religion of the Manichees. Added to this is the previous observation that they repeatedly came under imperial proscription so that their affairs (including diet) were a matter of enforced secrecy. The example of the enigmatical woman therefore becomes doubly appropriate to the case of the Manichees. Added to this there is the fact that Augustine had occasion to return to the example of that woman in another work ten to twenty years after writing the *Confessions*. Despite the time lapse, what he says on this later occasion about eating in secret is particularly appropriate to the Manichees:

> By such secrecy profane teachers (*nefarii doctores*) give a kind of seasoning to their poisons for the curious, that

91. *Ibid.*

92. Adeodatus, his son, was almost (*ferme*) fifteen at their baptism on April 24, 387 (*Conf.* 9, 6, 14), when Augustine was thirty-two and a half. This would mean that Augustine found himself a father at seventeen and a half years of age. He did not join the Manichees until he was nineteen.

> thereby they may imagine that they learn something
> great, because counted worthy of holding a secret, and
> may imbibe the more sweetly the folly which they regard
> as wisdom, the learning of which, as a thing prohibited,
> they are represented as stealing.[93]

As was mentioned, the religion of the Manichees was intensely concerned with dietary observations. All believers were supposed to be vegetarians because meat was considered tainted by the sexual generation which had produced it.[94] In addition, the priestly caste were not only vegetarians, but were forbidden to harm even trees and plants by plucking their fruits for consumption.[95] As a result, they depended on their disciples for the fruit and vegetables which sustained them. Augustine himself confesses that he spent some nine years carting food to the priests, or "elect" of the Manichees.[96] A further important element in the beliefs of the Manichees was the conviction that these priests could, during the very process of digestion itself, separate out the pure light element from the food that they ate, thus liberating it for its return to the Kingdom of Light.[97]

Despite his later ridiculing of this dietary aspect of Manicheism, it seems to have impressed Augustine to an extent which he himself did not realize. Thus, his stern

---

93. *Tractates on the Gospel according to St. John*, tractate 97, 2. This work was written in the period of 407-417.

94. *On the Morals of the Manichaeans* 15, 36-37; *Reply to Faustus* 30, 5.

95. *Conf.* 3, 10, 18.

96. *Conf.* 4, 1, 1.

97. *Conf.* 3, 10, 18.

self-examination on gluttony in the tenth book of the *Confessions* is supported by numerous citations from the Scriptures, yet when these are examined, they are seen not to be concerned with gluttony at all, but rather with religious sanctions in regard to diet.[98]

Another example also seems to substantiate the same conclusion about the enduring impact upon Augustine of the dietary aspect of Manicheism. This example compares two passages and finds surprising similarities. Thus, in the *Confessions* he ridicules the case of some priest of the Manichees eating a fig in order to liberate the light element from it and goes on to say of the same:

> Yea, in his prayers he shall assuredly groan and sigh forth particles of God, which particles of the high and true God should have remained bound in that fig unless they had been set free by the teeth and belly of some 'elect saint.'[99]

However, in the *On Christian Doctrine* which was written in 396, or about a year before Augustine started writing the *Confessions,* one is surprised to come across a remarkably similar passage which concerns, not an elect of the Manichees, but holy men of the Catholic Church. Even more astounding is Augustine's admission that he does not recognize the source of the feelings which he expresses:

98. *Conf.* 10, 31, 43–47. *Cf.* Leo C. Ferrari, 'The Gustatory Augustin,' *Augustiniana* 29 (1979) 304–315.

99. *Conf.* 3, 10, 18. *Cf. Reply to Faustus the Manichaean* 20, 11–13; *On the Morals of the Manichaeans* 15, 36 to 17, 62.

> And yet, I don't know why, I feel greater pleasure in contemplating holy men when I view them as the teeth of the Church (*quasi dentes Ecclesiae*), tearing men away from their errors, and bringing them into the Church's body, with all their harshness softened down, just as if they had been torn off and masticated by the teeth.[100]

Augustine's enduring preoccupation with what may be termed the alimentary aspects of experience need not remain entirely a mystery. Thanks to some valuable episodes in the *Confessions,* it is possible to gain some insights into earlier experiences of his life which would help explain this phenomenon. Thus, it would seem that when he was a child, exclusion from the family table was a means of punishing misconduct,[101] a practice which he himself later adopted to discipline the gossipy members of his little religious community.[102] Then too, during his childhood there were the various thefts of victuals, not only to eat himself, but also to win prestige among his friends, as evidenced by the thefts from the family's food supply[103] and also by the famous theft of the pears.[104] No wonder then that the outlawed Manichees with their secret banquets later so fascinated the Augustine of nineteen. Also, years afterwards, when writing the *Confessions,* the older Augustine still found tortured appeal in the above-

100. *On Christian Doctrine* 2, 6, 7.
101. *Conf.* 3, 11, 1.
102. Possidius *Vita* 22.
103. *Conf.* 1, 18, 30.
104. *Conf.* 2, 4–8.

cited image of the woman inviting passers-by to partake of stolen water and to eat bread in secret.

The *Confessions* also offers us even earlier alimentary experiences in Augustine's life; experiences whose very survival in recollection attests to their enduring impact. Most important of these was the incident of the excruciating stomach pains which he suffered as a boy; pains of such intensity as to bring him to death's door.[105] When he implored his mother for final baptism, the pains suddenly departed.[106] This traumatic experience offers a better understanding of Augustine's fearful reverence for the God who would destroy the belly[107] as also his stern self-examination in regard to food and drink in the tenth book of the *Confessions*.[108] One can also better understand why he seriously considered that his first sin might have been in crying for the breast.[109] Likewise too, his doctrine of Original Sin seems to have received substantiation from the observed behaviour of infants during breast-feeding (*Ibid.*).

Finally in the *Confessions* then, when summarizing his Manichean sojourn, Augustine compares that experience to a disappointing meal. Despite the sarcasm, from the very metaphor, as well as the above examples, it would appear that this aspect of the religion held an intense

105. *Conf.* 1, 11, 17.

106. One is reminded of the similar experience at Cassiciacum of the fierce tooth-ache. (*Conf.* 9, 4, 12.)

107. *Conf.* 10, 31, 43. *Cf. I Cor.* 6, 13.

108. *Conf.* 10, 31, 43–47.

109. *Conf.* 1, 7, 11.

31

fascination for Augustine, as has been seen. Consequently, when after some nine years he came to abandoning that sect, it would appear that for the scrupulous Augustine, a religious diet of such long duration was not so easily abandoned. Apparently, in his crisis of conscience, he found support in the Apostle Paul, whom the Manichees were so fond of quoting. Chapter eight of I Corinthians seems to have become particularly precious to Augustine at that time; a fact which is evidenced by his own observations. The chapter is concerned with the question of Christians eating food which had been offered to idols. Paul's observation that "food will not commend us to God" (*Op. cit* 8, 8), delighted the troubled Augustine; a fact which he long remembered. It was an answer from his beloved Paul which well applied to his own particular problem. Accordingly, some dozen years after the crisis he writes in the *Confessions:*

> And by Thy favour, I have heard this saying likewise, which I have much rejoiced in (*quam multum amavi*) 'Neither if we eat, are we the better; neither if we eat not, are we the worse;' which is to say, that neither shall the one make me to abound, nor the other to be wretched.[110]

(ii) "They served up to me dishes of glowing fantasies" (Conf. 3, 6, 10)

Another element of interest in Augustine's description of his entrapment by the Manichees concerns the sun and

110. *Conf.* 10, 31, 45. The quote is from *I Cor.* 8, 8.

moon which he depicts as being on those dishes that they served up to him (*Conf.* 3, 6, 10). Later on in the text Augustine describes the food on the dishes as glowing fantasies (*phantasmata splendida*) and confesses that he fed on them, though without either obtaining nourishment or enjoyment. He declares too, that while those heavenly bodies were beautiful works of God, they were not God himself; a denial which would have fallen painfully on the ears of the Manichees. Their conceptions of God and their counterpart of the Christian Trinity are well expressed by Faustus, an eminent Manichee, in a treatise which Augustine wrote while he was working on his *Confessions*. There follows then, what may be here entitled the basic Manichean Credo:

> We worship then, one deity under the threefold appellation of the Almighty God the Father and his son Christ, and the Holy Spirit. While these are one and the same, we believe also that the Father properly dwells in the highest or principal light, which Paul calls 'Light inaccessible' and the Son in his second or visible light. And as the Son is himself twofold according to the Apostle who speaks of Christ as the power of God and the wisdom of God, we believe that His power dwells in the sun, and his wisdom in the moon. We also believe that the Holy Spirit, the third majesty, has His seat and His home in the whole circle of the atmosphere. By His influence and spiritual infusion, the earth conceives and brings forth the mortal Jesus (*Jesus patabilis*), who, as hanging from every tree, is the life and salvation of men.[111]

111. *Reply to Faustus* 20, 2. The references to Paul are from *I Tim.* 6, 16 and *I Cor.*, 1, 24 respectively.

This extract shows why the Manichees held physical light in extreme reverence and worshipped the sun and moon and also explains why Augustine refers to them as setting before him on dishes, these two heavenly bodies. Furthermore, if we search other works of Augustine, besides the *Confessions,* we find some interesting details which would suggest that the heavens were also very much involved in his entrapment by the Manichees. Thus, as early as 386, or some dozen years before the writing of the *Confessions,* the work entitled *The Happy Life* contains some significant allusions to events in the heavens:

> From the age of nineteen, having read in the school of rhetoric that book of Cicero's called *Hortensius,* I was inflamed by such a great love of philosophy that I considered devoting myself to it at once. Yet I was not free of those mists (*nebulae*) which could confuse my course, and I confess that for quite a while I was led astray (*in errorem ducebar*), with my eyes fixed on those stars that sink in the ocean (*labentia in oceanum astra suspexi*). A childish superstition deterred me from thorough investigation (*nam et superstitio quaedam puerilis me ab ipsa inquisitione terrebat*), and, as soon as I was more courageous, I threw off the darkness and learned to trust more in men that taught than in those that ordained obedience, having myself encountered persons to whom the very light, seen by their eyes, apparently was an object of highest and even divine veneration.[112]

Recalling that the section of *The Happy Life* from which the above extract is taken, concerns the sea-voyage to the port of philosophy, then Augustine is saying that he

112. *The Happy Life* 1, 4.

was led astray during that voyage and into Manicheism by having his eyes fixed on the stars that sink into the ocean. Immediately following this is the intriguing detail of having been literally terrified by a childish superstition (*superstitio quaedam puerilis me . . . terrebat*). Furthermore, not only does this most interesting detail follow immediately upon the reference to the stars sinking into the ocean, but there is the conjunction *nam,* which would explain the fact of being led astray by the added reason of terror. From this one can deduce the following sequence of events: (i) the young Augustine was led astray, (ii) the reason being that he was watching the stars, and (iii) he was so engaged because he was terrified by a childish superstition.

While there have been some ingenious but implausible explanations for that terror and childish superstition,[113] the above description would seem to clearly link such reactions to some phenomenon in the heavens.. The most obvious explanation would seem to be the Manichees with their legends of the divinity of the sun and moon. But one would have to be very gullible to believe that at the age of nineteen, Augustine was himself so gullible. In any case, the reference is to stars (*astra*) and not to either sun or moon. Furthermore, of the two, the sun would be the better candidate for such a hoax. But the reference to stars clearly implies that it was question of some nocturnal phenomenon. One is therefore led to conclude that it must have been some phenomenon of unprecedented awesome-

113. Courcelle *Recherches* pp. 64–65.

ness in the night sky. However, before examining this question further, it would be advisable to look at Augustine's other relevant accounts of his conversion to Manicheism.

Two other useful descriptions of that conversion are to be found in *The Profit of Believing* of 391/2 and therefore some half dozen years after the previous account. In the first of these later descriptions, there is again an explicit mention of terror and superstition:

> For, what else forced me for almost nine years, during which time I rejected the religion which my parents had implanted in me as a child, to follow these men the Manichees and diligently to listen to them, save that they said we were terrified by superstition (*nos superstitioni terreri*), and that faith was demanded of us before reason, while they, on the other hand, were forcing faith on no one without first hunting for and disentangling the truth.[114]

What is lacking here, is the explicit connection of the source of that terror with the stars, as was seen in the text from *The Happy Life*. However, on the reasonable assumption that it is indeed question of the same experience in both cases, then the present extract adds some significant details, first of which is the implication of company by the words: *nos superstitioni terreri*. Just how large this company was, is a matter for conjecture. However, in the case of some awesome apparition in the night sky, then one can assume that the entire human race

114. *Op. cit.* 1, 2.

was involved. Next, the second significant detail is that the Manichees were *not* terrified. Indeed, from the above excerpt, it would follow that they claimed to have some "rational" explanation for the phenomenon which was the cause of widespread terror. Finally, one can appreciate that the mention of reason would have had added appeal to the young Augustine, fresh from the Hortensius experience.

However, before pursuing further the awesome aspect of the phenomenon, it would be helpful to examine the other allusion to terror in *The Profit of Believing*. This allusion is to be found following the extract already used and refers to the Manichees trapping the unwary, like birdcatchers who spread their sticky birdlime on tree-branches. In such a manner, says Augustine, was he taken in by those deceivers. The Meagher translation reads as follows:

> And so they did to us what deceitful bird-catchers are wont to do, who fix lime-smeared branches near water to deceive thirsty birds. These men cover over and conceal in any way they can the other surrounding waters or even ward off the birds by formidable devices (*formidolosis molitionibus*), so that they fall into snares, not through choice, but out of pure need.[115]

In regard to the translation, it is important to point out that the adjective *formidolosis* would seem to imply a stronger emotion than that described by the word "formidable" which is used to translate it. More appropriate

115. *On the Profit of Believing* 1, 2.

renditions would seem to be "fearful" or even "terrifying," either of which would place the emotion in the category under present consideration. Next, the word *molitio,* meaning a putting in motion, poses problems. To translate it as "device," as has been done, might make one first think of a scarecrow, but the word *molitio* itself implies some kind of rotation, like the waving of large bright objects to terrify the birds. However, the intriguing question arises as to what could be an equivalent in the case of the Manichees.

Two authors greatly admired by Augustine at different stages of his life, would seem to contain some helpful hints. Cicero, author of the *Hortensius,* uses *molitio* for the act of making in the sense of the creation of the world.[116] Taken in this sense, one can speculate that Augustine's terror was not merely connected with some phenomenon in the night sky, but also involved the Manichean cosmogony. Further, in conjunction with the earlier extract from *The Profit of Believing,* and the Manichees' championing of reason, one could conclude that they claimed to have an explanation for the terrifying phenomenon; an explanation based on their cosmogony.

The second author admired by Augustine is Ambrose, who uses *molitio* in the sense of a grinding,[117] which implies a turning, and (in the present case), a turning of the nocturnal heavens.

Interestingly enough, modern research has uncovered a possible explanation for what may well have been in-

116. *De natura deorum* 1, 8, 19.
117. *Sermo 29*

tended by this strange phrase *formidolosis molitionibus.*
It would appear that the Manichees believed in a gigantic
cosmic wheel composed of the twelve parts of the zodiac as
spokes, and which, like a water-wheel with its buckets
drew the separated light element up from the earth and
deposited it in the moon.[118] Therefore, it would appear
that they believed that the sun and the moon together with
the milky way and the twelve constellations were all set in
motion to aid in extracting the sacred light element from
the darkness of earthly matter and transporting it, via the
moon and the sun, back to the Kingdom of Light inaccessi-
ble.[119] Apparently, Augustine was not unfamiliar with this
conception. Thus, in his treatise *Reply to Faustus* of
397/8, when speaking of the various gods of the Manichees, he mentions one who "in his circuit of the heavens
(*in coelo circumiens*) gathers by his spokes (*radiis suis . . .
colligit*) the members of your god from cesspools."[120]

So much then for the allusions to superstitious terror
in Augustine's account of his conversion to Manicheism.
As far as I have been able to ascertain, *The Profit of
Believing* of 391/2 contains the last of such allusions in his
writings. Even so, being written nearly twenty years after
the conversion to Manicheism, *The Profit of Believing* of-

118. Widengren *Op. cit.* pp. 55–56; Burkitt *Op. cit.* p. 43.

119. A. V. Williams Jackson, *Researches in Manicheism; with Special Reference to the Turfan Fragments,* 1932, pp. 10, 237, 294. *Cf. Man-
ichäische Handschriften der Staatlichen Museen,* Berlin, Band I, *Kep-
halaia,* Kap. 69, pp. 166–169.

120. *Reply to Faustus* 20, 10. I have substituted "spokes" for
"beams" in the Stothert translation which seems to imply that the sun is
intended.

fers eloquent testimony to the enduring impact of that terror.

As to what could have possibly been its cause, I have tried to show elsewhere[121] that its source was the sudden and unexpected appearance in the night sky over Carthage of what was later to become known as Halley's Comet. Thanks to the assistance of Dr. Bryan Andrew of the Astrophysics Branch of the National Research Council of Canada, I have been able to ascertain that the Comet was first visible in the night sky over Carthage about March 1 (Julian time), 374, reaching maximum brightness about April 1 and fading from view about the end of the month. This means that for about two months, this eerie spectacle was present in the night sky, so that Augustine along with everyone else, could not but have seen it. With a luminous tail extending through some 40 or 50 degrees of vision, it must have been a terrifying spectacle indeed, particularly since no one, (with the possible exception of the Manichees) knew where it came from, or what it portended.

Regarding the question of chronological accord with the date of Augustine's entry into Manicheism, we have his repeated remembrance that this occurred in his nineteenth year.[122] According to Courcelle's calculations,[123] this

121. Leo C. Ferrari, 'Halley's Comet of 374; New Light upon Augustine's Conversion to Manicheism,' *Augustiniana* 27 (1977) 139–150.

122. *Conf.* 3, 4, 7; 3, 6, 10 & 4, 1, 1.

123. *Recherches* p. 78. I had previously maintained the date-range of a year earlier, on the basis of an interpretation of the phrase "in my nineteenth year" as naming the year prior to the nineteenth birthday. (*art. cit.* pp. 142–143). However, "from the age of nineteen" would more commonly mean during the year after the nineteenth birthday.

would extend from November 373 to November 374, which is in perfect accord with the above appearance of the comet during March and April, 374. Therefore, from the point of view of chronological accord there is an impressive congruence obtained by my so-called "Halley's Comet Hypothesis."

To further appreciate the impact that the unheralded appearance of that comet would have made, it is helpful to recall that the event occurred in an age long before the arrival of electric lights had blinded man to the majestic grandeur of the starry vault. Moreover, there was the ominous reputation attaching to comets, since with their periodic nature not being known, they were commonly regarded as eerie intruders upon the ordered cycles of nature.

Added to the above generalities were the particular dispositions of Augustine himself. His early dialogues show him as an enthralled star-gazer who reckoned all the beauties of earth as of little worth compared with the expansive grandeur of the starry vault.[124] No doubt, one of the important sources of this enthralment was the *Aeneid* of his beloved Virgil; a work which had captivated his imagination from his earliest school days.[125] Thus, it is most significant that the first excerpt from *The Happy Life,* cited above, and referring to his having been led into error by watching the stars that sink into the ocean, is a line adapted from the third book of the *Aeneid;* where it is

124. *Soliloquies* 1, 1.

125. *Conf.* 1, 13, 20–22. *Cf.* The presence of Virgil's *Aeneid* at Cassiciacum (*Answer to Skeptics* 2, 4, 10).

said of Palinurus: *sidera cuncta notat tacito labentia coelo*
("all the stars he scanned as they slid through the quiet
sky") (3.515).

While the *Aeneid* itself contains numerous references
to stars, many of these references concern preternatural
events which must have been well known to Augustine by
the year 374. Thus, there is the arrow of Acestes, which
shot high into the sky, took fire, burned itself out and
vanished. As the poet informs us, this was considered an
omen of utmost significance for the future (5.519–527).
This portentous omen also reminds the poet of the similar
case of comets: "often, a star dislodges itself from heaven
and shoots across it, trailing a long-haired flame."
(5.527–528).

More immediately relevant to Augustine's own case,
was the omen granted the aged father of Aeneas, Anchises,
who was all but decided to stay behind and be slaughtered
by the Greeks in the downfall of Troy. But his last prayer
to the gods for a sign did not go unanswered:

> The old man had hardly spoken when from our left
> came
> A sudden crash of thunder, and a shooting star slid
> down
> The sky's dark face, drawing a trail of light behind it.
> We watched that star as it glided high over the palace
> roof
> And blazing a path, burned its brightness deep in the
> woods of Ida; when it was gone, it left in its wake a long
> furrow of light, and a sulphurous smoke spread widely
> over the terrain.[126]

126. *Op. cit.* 2.692–698. The passages are from the C. Day Lewis
translation.

Such are a few of the more obvious literary passages which would have heightened Augustine's apprehensions when the comet appeared over Carthage in early March, 374. As to why the Manichees would have tended to regard the event with jubilation, and so be able to give a "rational" explanation of it, we have but to recall their belief about the divinity of the sun and the moon and the importance of all the heavenly bodies in the separation of the sacred light element and its transportation back to the Kingdom of Light. For them therefore, the comet of 374 would have been an occasion, not of abject terror, but of great rejoicing. An additional factor of no small importance was the approaching centenary of the martyrdom of Mani in 276/277; a martyrdom which they celebrated each year with the feast of the Bema.[127] Therefore, on the basis of their religious beliefs, they would have been strongly inclined to regard the comet as a messenger of hope. They could well afford therefore, to scoff at the agitated nonbelievers who were terrified by "a childish superstition," while they themselves had a "rational" explanation for the eerie apparition.

Therefore, on the basis of his mysterious references to "being terrified by a childish superstition," as well as the factor of exact chronological accord and the beliefs of the Manichees, it would appear that the comet of 374 was a decisive factor in Augustine's conversion to Manicheism, a creed which was to claim his allegiance for at least the next nine years. Interestingly enough, and in a complementary

---

127. *Against the Epistle of Manichaeus called Fundamental* 8, 9.

fashion, there is strong evidence that another celestial phenomenon contributed to his disenchantment with that sect.

In the fifth book of the *Confessions* Augustine is concerned with the events of his twenty-ninth year (*Conf.* 5, 3, 3). According to his account, it was in that year that Carthage (where he was then teaching) was visited by the celebrated Manichean bishop, Faustus. Augustine recalls that he had been looking forward to his arrival with "but too great eagerness" (*nimis extento desiderio. Conf.* 5, 6, 10). The immediate reason for this is not far to seek. Augustine had raised some difficult questions which his co-religionists were unable to answer. They bade him await the arrival of the famous Faustus, who would solve his problems. (*Ibid.*).

As to the nature of those difficulties of Augustine, the manifold examples in the text[128] offer bountiful evidence of the fact that it was question of the astronomers' (*philosophi*) proven ability to predict certain celestial phenomena, and particularly eclipses:

> For with their understanding and the capacity which Thou hast bestowed upon them they search out these things; and much have they found out, and foretold many years before,—the eclipses of those luminaries, the sun and moon, and on what day, at what hour, and from how many particular points they were likely to come.[129]

128. *Conf.* 5, 3, 3-6.
129. *Conf.* 5, 3, 4.

44

In addition, there is repeated evidence of the fact that Augustine had personally witnessed the fulfilment of these astronomers' predictions: "Nor did their calculations fail them; and it came to pass even as they foretold." (*op. cit.* 5, 3, 6). Recalling that the year of Faustus' visit was 383, it is significant that there had been a solar eclipse on January 12, 381, whose central path lay about 1700 miles south of Carthage,[130] which made its occurrence quite verifiable at that city, where Augustine was then residing. In addition, there had been another solar eclipse on September 8, 378, with a central path some 1100 miles south of Carthage. The only previous occasion on which Augustine could have witnessed a solar eclipse would have been on March 15, 359, when he would have been some five years old. The solar eclipses of 378 and 381 were therefore without precedence in his mature years.

But as a practising Manichee, Augustine had been worshipping the sun and moon, for the reasons already seen, in what has been called the basic Manichean Credo (see above).[131] However, the humbling fact that solar eclipses had been successfully predicted in Augustine's own milieu, brought these supposedly divine beings down to what could be termed in modern parlance, mere matter in motion, and indeed, motion subject to predictable laws. Furthermore, in terms of the beliefs of the Manichees, the

130. For these details, see my 'Astronomy and Augustine's Break with the Manichees,' *Revue des Etudes Augustiniennes* 19 (1973) 263–276.

131. The Manichees prayed to the sun during the day, and to the moon at night. (*De haeresibus* 46).

eclipses meant the supreme blasphemy that the power of the Son (in the sun) united with the wisdom of the Son (in the moon) produced darkness![132] Such blasphemous thoughts were urged upon the inquiring Augustine by the events described. According to the Manichean code of belief, to entertain such thoughts was an act of supreme sinfulness.[133] That Augustine was impatiently awaiting the arrival of Faustus is not merely understandable, but is also a testimony to the sincerity of his Manichean beliefs in what proved to be their unsuccessful confrontation with the science of his times.

Before leaving the subject of Augustine's conversion to Manicheism, there is another conversion which appears to have occurred soon after the former one. This latter introduced him to a system of beliefs which even seems to have outlived his allegiance to Manicheism, thereby suggesting a stronger hold over him.[134] I am referring to his conversion to astrology, which, with its preternatural attitude towards the heavens, was apparently favoured by the Manichees.[135] As Augustine himself confesses, he became an ardent student of the books of the astrologers

---

132. *Cf. Reply to Faustus* 20, 8.

133. Jes P. Asmussen, *Manichaean Literature; Representative Texts from Middle Persian and Parthian Writings,* 1975, pp. 70–77. Burkitt, *Op. cit.* 51ff.

134. See my 'Augustine and Astrology,' *Laval Théologique et Philosophique* 33 (1977) 241–245, especially pp. 246–248.

135. Prosper Alfaric *Les écritures manichéennes,* I, Paris, 1918, p. 35; also, Francois Decret, *Aspects du manichéisme dans l'Afrique romaine; les controverses de Fortunatus, Faustus et Felix avec saint Augustin,* Paris, 1970, pp. 35–36, 228.

and with such dedication that even the best arguments of his closest friends could not convince him of the futility of his studies.[136]

Due in part to the attention which Augustine's Manichean sojourn has received, both in his writings and in the resulting studies of them, his prolonged dedication to astrology seems to have passed almost unnoticed. Consequently, except for a few Dutch scholars,[137] this aspect of his life has been greatly underrated.[138] But if we take careful note of the Firminius episode in the *Confessions* (7, 6, 8-10), it would seem that Augustine had even become involved in the dark art of astrology to the extent of having become a practising astrologer.[139] Furthermore, it is my conviction that Augustine has left us a thinly disguised account of this aspect of his life elsewhere in his writings.[140]

What seems to have transpired however, is that as Augustine delved deeper into those books of the astrologers, he also had to acquire a greater knowledge of astronomy. Consequently, as he says elsewhere, he acquired a good knowledge of astronomy quite early in

---

136. *Conf.* 4, 3, 4-6.

137. L. C. P. J. De Vreese, *Augustinus en de Astrologie,* Maastricht, 1933; E. Hendrikx, OESA, 'Astrologie, Waarzeggerij en Parapsychologie bij Augustinus,' *Augustiniana* 4 (1954) 109-136.

138. Even Brown (p. 57) mentions offhandedly that Augustine "dabbled in astrology."

139. Thus, Firminius asks Augustine what he saw of his (Firminius') future in the stars: ("quid mihi secundum suas quas constellationes appellant videretur") (*Conf.* 7, 6, 8). *Cf.* Prosper Alfaric, *L'évolution intellectuelle de saint Augustin,* I, Paris, 1918, p. 22.

140. See my 'The Peculiar Appendage of Augustine's Enarratio in Psalmum LXI,' *Augustiniana* 28 (1978) 18-33.

life.[141] Apparently, like his interest in astrology, his growing knowledge of astronomy enjoyed a peaceful coexistence with his dedication to Manicheism until the solar eclipses of 378 and 381 forced a drastic confrontation between two vastly different appraisals of the sun and moon.[142] As was seen, the resulting crisis contributed to his disenchantment with Manicheism and his later abandonment of it.

It would appear then, that the comet of 374 not only precipitated Augustine's conversion to Manicheism, but eventually converted him also to a zealous pursuit of astrology, which in turn led him to delve deeper into astronomy. Apparently, it was his ongoing interest in this last-mentioned discipline that forcefully brought the anticipated eclipses of 378 and 381 to his attention. The fulfilment of both scientific predictions had disastrous implications for his Manichean attitude to both heavenly bodies involved, and for reasons which have been seen. The resulting religious crisis left him waiting with "but too great eagerness" for the coming of the widely acclaimed Manichean bishop, Faustus, who (so he had been assured) would explain away his problems. As subsequent events proved, such was not the case, and so Manicheism lost the allegiance of one of the most brilliant minds of history.

Before leaving the topic of astrology, it is noteworthy

141. *Epistula 55* 4, 6–11. As he says: 'haec in studiis puerilibus didici.' Regarding which, it should be noted that while 'puer' was strictly said of youths of seventeen, it was often used for men much older.

142. Presumably too, as an astrologer, he would have been more concerned with the stars than with the sun and moon.

that here, yet again, Augustine's initial interest in the subject seems to have grown out of his preoccupation with the origin of evil. Such is implied in the *Confessions* (4, 3, 4), where he first introduces the topic of astrology and quotes the practitioners of that art as telling him: "the cause of thy sin is inevitably determined in the heavens," and "this did Venus, or Saturn, or Mars." The purpose of all this is, as Augustine goes on to say: "that man, forsooth, flesh and blood, and proud corruption, may be blameless."[143]

143. *Cf. On Continence.* 14.

III THE CONVERSIONS TO CATHOLICISM

I use the plural "conversions" here because I believe that there are good reasons for distinguishing more than one, as will be seen. However, before embarking on this project, it is important to emphasize the fact that in his earlier works, Augustine regarded his conversion to Catholicism as the culmination of a lengthy quest for *philosophia:* a quest which stemmed ultimately from the Hortensius episode. Further, it would seem that the only interruption was his sojourn of some nine years among the Manichees. Yet, as has also been seen, it was basically the very same search for *philosophia* which enticed him into this heresy, so that this too becomes yet another stage in his ongoing quest for that same wisdom of philosophy.

However, this enduring continuity is not to be found in the narrative of the *Confessions.* There, the ardent desire for *philosophia* certainly initiates the pilgrimage towards the truth, but its continuing presence becomes unacknowledged in the subsequent story. Yet its enduring influence is demonstrated by the fact that the importance of the ardent search for *philosophia* re-emerges towards the end of the story, to play an important role in the concluding events of Augustine's well-known conversion.[144]

144. This concerns the discovery of the "books of the Platonists": *Conf.* 7, 9, 13–15; 7, 11, 13–15; 7, 20, 26.

However, between the beginning and the end of the lengthy process, the guiding light of *philosophia* goes largely unacknowledged.

On the other hand, its presence throughout the narrative would certainly have drastically altered the nature of the *Confessions* as we have come to know it, perhaps also narrowing its appeal considerably to "intellectual" readers. One may be tempted to see this as one reason for the omission of *philosophia* from the continuum of the narrative. However, I believe that there is another and more fundamental reason for that omission; a reason which lies in the nature of a later and less known conversion of Augustine, as will be seen.

(i) The Conversion-Scene of the Confessions

That Augustine was indeed profoundly and permanently converted to Catholicism is a basic truth beyond all reasonable doubt. However my researches of more recent years have led me to follow in the footsteps of the eminent Courcelle in regarding the well-known conversion-scene of the *Confessions* as extremely suspect.[145] Furthermore, on the basis of my own findings I would have to agree with him that the very manner of presentation of that scene in the garden of Milan is to be understood as *un mode de présentation romanesque*,[146] or a certain romanticizing of reality.

145. *Recherches* pp. 188–202.
146. *Op. cit.* p. 200.

That scene, which constitutes the climax of the work as a whole, has certain salient features which are worth recalling here. Earlier in the eighth book, Augustine has been visited by a certain Pontitianus who relates to him a conversion which is remarkably similar to the one which is about to be described to the reader of the *Confessions*. This story has the effect upon Augustine of precipitating an inner conflict of extreme intensity which is described with consummate artistry. After the departure of Pontitianus, becoming even more embroiled in inner turmoil, Augustine withdraws with his closest friend, Alypius, to the garden of their house. There, the continuation of the violent struggle of self against self eventually causes Augustine to cast himself down on the ground in tearful desperation. He happens to be under a certain fig-tree (*sub quadam fici arbore*), bitterly weeping over his persistent resistance to divine grace, when he suddenly hears a voice from the neighbouring house (*ecce audio vocem de vicina domo*). It is the voice of a boy or a girl, and chants repetitively (*cum cantu dicentis et crebro repentis quasi pueri an puellae, nescio*). It is repeatedly chanting the now-famous words: *tolle lege, tolle lege*—"take up and read, take up and read."

Interpreting this as a divine command (*nihil aliud interpretans, nisi divinitus mihi iubere*) to take up and consult the volume of Paul which he had been reading before the visit of Pontitianus, Augustine ceases weeping and arises from the ground. He goes to that section of the garden nearer the house, where he had left his friend Alypius and the volume of Paul. He opens the volume and reads the very first passage upon which his vision falls. It is the now-famous passage of *Romans* 13, 13-14:

> Not in rioting and drunkenness, not in chambering and wantonness, not in strife and envying; but put ye on the Lord Jesus Christ, and make not provision for the flesh, to fulfill the lusts thereof.[147]

The reading of this passage has the immediate effect of infusing Augustine's heart with a light of security which causes the oppressive gloom of doubt to vanish entirely. Consistently with the example of Pontitianus' little story, Alypius too is converted by reading from the same volume. They go into the house and recount to Augustine's mother, Monica, the miraculous events which have just transpired. There is great rejoicing. Finally, as Augustine pointedly observes, he is at last standing on that very same rule of faith (*stans in ea regular fidei*) upon which his mother had seen him standing in a prophetic dream some dozen years previously.[148]

Thanks to the consummate artistry involved, the entire conversion account is possessed of such dramatic impact that, as O'Meara has so well observed,[149] it stays with the reader long after all the other details of the *Confessions* have been forgotten. And this of course was precisely Augustine's intention. Some sixteen centuries after the

147. *Conf.* 8, 12, 29.

148. See my 'Monica on the Wooden Ruler (Conf. 3, 11, 19),' *Augustinian Studies* 6 (1975) 193-205.

149. P. 59 in 'Arripui, aperui et legi,' *Augustinus Magister* I (1954) 59-65.

53

events described, the *Confessions* continues to fulfil its author's intention of raising the minds and the hearts of its readers to God and His saving grace.[150]

This primary purpose of the work is so obvious as to be easily overlooked. All the more important therefore, is the need to stress it, particularly since it is not to be identified with the scholar's principal interest in the work. It cannot be sufficiently emphasized that as students of the *Confessions*, we tend to assume all too easily that it was written primarily to be analyzed and dissected in the solitude of a study. Nothing could be further from the truth. The *Confessions* was primarily written to be *read* and indeed, *read aloud and in company* . This observation is particularly relevant to the controversial phrase: *ecce audio vocem de vicina domo*—"behold, I hear a voice from the neighbouring house." In the centuries before Gutenberg, when books were rare and reading was a highly social event, those words would have fallen far less incongruously upon the ears of the hearers than they do upon the minds of modern readers. The world of difference is that today, reading is primarily a silent and private pastime. Today's silent readers would have been just as much a source of unending puzzlement to the hearers of antiquity as the silently reading Ambrose was to the highly vocal Augustine.[151]

Recalling also that Augustine was primarily educated to excel in rhetoric, or public speaking, one is therefore closer to the original perspective in regarding the *Confes-*

150. *Conf.* 10, 3, 4–6.

151. *Conf.* 6, 3, 3. See also my ' "Ecce audis voceris de vicina domo" (*Conf.* 8, 12, 29),' *Augustiniana* (in press).

sions not primarily as a book for private study (whether academic or spiritual), but primarily as a script for a dramatic reading and indeed a reading whose primary purpose was communal edification. One internal sign of this intention is that of the vocal and auditory orientations of the work as a whole. It is understandable therefore that the word "to hear" (*audire*) and its variants occur some one hundred and eighty-three times in the *Confessions*. Likewise, "voice" (*vox*) and its cognates are found one hundred and thirty-seven times.[152]

These various considerations place the problem of the voice which Augustine claims to have heard in a completely different perspective. While this new perspective does not dispose of the problems associated with the incident, it does deprive it of much of the pretentiousness that it has acquired in the modern perspective.

This contemporary attitude accounts for a lot of the attention that the "voice" has acquired among modern scholars. In 1958, Marrou, in his "La querelle autour du Tolle lege,"[153] tried to touch on some of the more prominent of the emergent opinions, with special reference to

152. The source of these and other such statistics on the words of the *Confessions* is an *Index Verborum* to the work, recently constructed at the School of Computer Science of The University of New Brunswick. The computer programming, systems design and implementation were effected by Prof. Rodney H. Cooper and Programmer Analyst, Mr. Peter Ruddock. All the typing was done by Debra Ruddock. Text proofreading and editing were performed by Prof. J. Robert Smith of UNB's Classics Dept. and myself of the Philosophy Dept. of St. Thomas University, which also provided some funding for text-editing.

153. *Revue d'histoire ecclésiastique* 53 (1958) 47–57.

that of the doyen of students of the *Confessions*—the erudite Courcelle. In concluding the article, Marrou regretted that the heated debate had ever arisen, being excessively concerned, in his opinion, with such a small episode: an episode almost without importance, a mere detail—*un petit épisode, presque sans importance, un détail. (Art. cit.* p. 57).

In the modern perspective, such an opinion voiced in scholarly circles is like presenting the proverbial red flag to the bull. Understandably therefore, such a verdict, especially coming from a scholar of Marrou's stature, has stimulated, rather than stemmed, the flow of studies on the conversion-scene in general, and on the "tolle lege" episode in particular.

For all its sincerity, Marrou's verdict seems to have ignored two important aspects of the question. First, to the modern mind, anyone that claims to have been guided by some mysterious "voice" becomes the immediate object of intense suspicion. Secondly, and more important in a study of the *Confessions,* is the undeniable fact that the "tolle lege" episode is the grand climax of the entire autobiography of the work. As such, it is anything but *un petit épisode presque sans importance, un détail.*

However, this opinion of Marrou appears less exaggerated when it is recalled that in our age with its passion for facts, there are those extremists who would commit the entire *Confessions* to trial over the mere detail of whether or not Augustine really did hear a real voice in the garden at Milan on the occasion of his conversion. To put the entire work on trial over the authenticity—the *Glauwbürdigkeit*—of one little detail in it (no matter how impor-

56

tant to the internal drama), does, after all show a lamentable lack of perspective.

Such an exigency would demonstrate yet again that reality is simple only to the simple-minded. With regard to the factual aspects of the *Confessions*, Courcelle's warning against *l'exactitude sténographique* (*Recherches* p. 38), is most important. There are those who would seem convinced that Augustine was constantly followed around from the earliest years by the stenographers of later life. As a result, they imagine that every little detail was immediately committed to writing, the very moment that it transpired, to be used in later years by the author of the *Confessions*. With these various observations made, it may be somewhat safer to approach the delicate subject of the factuality of the conversion-scene in the eighth book of the *Confessions*.

Since Harnack's *Augustins Confessionen* of 1888, which first questioned the sheer factuality of the entire autobiographical section of the work, the conversion-scene has been at the centre of the controversy. Regarding this scene as a whole, few have been willing to follow Courcelle's opinion that it is a romanticizing of reality. Most have felt safer in adhering closely to the letter of the text, with some even opting for *l'exactitude sténographique*. These latter may be called the "Historicists" for whom every event of the *Confessions* is an historical event and transpired exactly as described. Courcelle however, particularly with the first edition of his *Recherches* in 1950, became the champion of the opposed school of the "Fictionalists" for whom the reality of Augustine's conversion as depicted in the *Confessions* is embellished with concrete details derived not from lived experience according to *l'exactitude sténographique,* but from the dramatic exigencies of the work.

Thus, to take an interesting detail, there is the fig-tree under which Augustine casts himself down upon the ground. Courcelle did not hesitate (p. 193) to identify this fig-tree with the fig-tree under which Christ saw Nathanael (*John* 1, 48). Accordingly, for Courcelle, it represents *l'ombrage mortel des péchés du genre humain*—the deadly darkness of human sin. (*Ibid.*).

Buchheit's fine study of 1968[154] demonstrated in depth and detail, how the reputation of the fig-tree in antiquity widely warranted just such an interpretation. Furthermore, he also showed how the fig-tree, understood in its popular association with sexual concupiscence, has a very purposeful presence, not only in the garden-scene, but also in the entire eighth book of the *Confessions*. All of this, demonstrated yet again, the careful craftsmanship with which the work was constructed.

In the more recent past, it seemed to me that there was possible a completely different approach to the question of the factuality of the conversion-scene of the *Confessions*. By modern reckoning, the conversion of Augustine occurred late in the year 386. The *Confessions* was written somewhere in the time-range 397–401. This means that there are at least ten years between the actual conversion and the description of it in the *Confessions*. Augustine's

154. Vinzenz Buchheit, 'Augustinus unter dem Feigenbaum; (Zu Conf. VIII),' *Vigiliae Christianae* 22 (1968), 257-271.

many works written in the time-period 386–401 therefore constitute a potential source of valuable evidence on the question at issue. The problem is how to extract this evidence in a useable form.

The most obvious approach is to search for references to the event. After all, as Merki well observed, the Hortensius episode has a factuality beyond dispute, as evidenced by the many occasions on which Augustine refers to it in his later writings.[155] Since the conversion to Catholicism was immensely more important to him, one can therefore confidently expect that many more references would validate its authenticity, even to the extent of confirming many details of the conversion-scene of the eighth book.

However, while the solid fact of Augustine's conversion permeates even the earliest writings, there is precious little to substantiate the details of the conversion-scene. One possible explanation for this omission is that the occasion for such references just did not present itself.[156] Considering that Augustine probably excelled in nothing so much as seizing the initiative, as his many triumphant debates amply demonstrate, the previous reason for the omission seems remarkably inadequate.

For those searching Augustine's earlier works for confirming details of the conversion-scene, an encouraging detail would seem to be presented in the description of ex-

155. P. H. Merki, 'Tolle, lege! Interpretation zu Augustinus, Confessiones VIII, 5–12,' *Zeitschrift für die Höhere Schule,* (München), 13 (1967) 168–183), especially p. 179ff.

156. A. Solignac, p. 549 of 'Notes complémentaires' in *Les Confessions,* vol. 14 in *Oeuvres de Saint Augustin,* Paris, 1962.

citedly seizing upon the writings of Paul in the *Answer to the Skeptics* of 386.[157] Surely this is the very same incident as the detail of the famous conversion-scene where Augustine also seizes upon the volume of Paul, with the resulting reading which effects his final conversion. This is an opinion which even seems to have won the support of Courcelle.[158]

However, of the five uses of the verb "to seize" (*arripere*) in the *Confessions,* there are not one, but two, concerned with the writings of Paul (7, 21, 27 and 8, 12, 29). The first of these events is that which is depicted as the result of the discovery of the so-called "books of the Platonists,"[159] while in the *Against the Skeptics* the same action is attributed to the reading of "certain plenteous books" (*libri quidam pleni*).[160] It would be reasonable therefore to regard these as descriptions of one and the same event. However, to identify this latter episode with the seizing of the volume of Paul in the conversion-scene of the *Confessions* would seem to involve one in a blatant defiance of all the contextual evidence of both descriptions.

In the first place, besides the fact that both descriptions are separated by a considerable distance in the text of the *Confessions,* there is the added consideration that they each proceed from quite different causes. The former is

157. *Op. cit.* 2, 2, 5; *Cf. The Happy Life,* 1, 4.

158. *Recherches,* pp. 157–8, 168–9, 199, n. 1, 308–309. See also his 'Le visage de philosophie,' *Revue des Etudes Anciennes* 70 (1968) 110–120.

159. *Conf.* 7, 9, 13 and 20, 26 - 21, 27.

160. *Op. cit* 2, 2, 5.

the result of reading the books of the Platonists, while the latter is in obedience to the mysterious voice. Again, when one examines the intervening text in the *Confessions,* it becomes evident that no Courcellean chronological regress can be invoked to identify the two descriptions of seizing upon Paul's writings. Thus, after the first description, Augustine describes the many difficulties and dangers that still lie ahead before he can reach the land of peace:

> For it is one thing, from the mountain's wooded summit to see the land of peace, and not to find the way thither—in vain to attempt impassable ways, opposed and waylaid by fugitives and deserters . . . and another to keep to the way that leads thither, guarded by the host of the heavenly army.[161]

He goes on to say how these things did "sink into my bowels" (*mihi inviscerebantur*) as he read Paul and meditated upon God's creation and "feared greatly." All this however, is a far cry from the triumphant sequel to the conversion-scene with all its rejoicing and Augustine's standing at last upon that rule of faith (*Conf.* 8, 12, 30), when he had finally reached that land of peace.

Furthermore, after the first description of seizing Paul's writings at the end of the seventh book, as one reads on into the eighth book, it becomes abundantly clear that Augustine was still far from the light of security that was to flood his heart after the conversion-scene at the end of that book: "as for my temporal life, all things were uncertain, and my heart had to be purged from the old

---

161. *Conf.* 7, 21, 27. *Cf. Against the Skeptics* 2, 2, 6.

leaven."[162] Chief among the relevant details is his visit with Simplicianus to inquire how to walk on the way that led to God (*Ibid.*). Later on in the eighth book there is another visit; this time of Pontitianus to Augustine's abode, when he discovers the book of Paul's writings on a table (8, 6, 14). Not only is this consequent upon the first seizing of Paul's writings at the end of the seventh book, but there is yet another confirmatory detail in Augustine's reply to the surprise of Pontitianus: "I told him that I bestowed much pains upon these writings" (*Ibid.*). This also tallies with the observation in the *Answer to the Skeptics:* "I read the whole book with the greatest attention and care" (*perlegi totum intentissime atque cautissime*) (*Op. cit, 2, 2, 5*). Furthermore, what manner of reading, more than this, could stand in greater contrast both to the random choice and to the reading of a mere two verses, as occurs in the conversion-scene, after which also, there is no dejection, but rather rejoicing.[163]

Finally on the two descriptions in the *Confessions* of seizing upon the writings of Paul, there are their separate, but corresponding roles in the plan of the work. The seventh book is concerned with liberating Augustine from his materialism (7, 1, 1), thanks mainly to the discovery of the "books of the Platonists." The climax of the seventh book then becomes the seizing upon the writings of Paul.[164] In like manner, and as Buchheit's fine study[165]

162. *Conf.* 8, 1, 1. The allusion is to *I Cor.* 5, 7.

163. *Cf.* J. J. O'Meara, 'Plotinus and Augustine; Exegesis of Contra Academicos 2, 5,' *Revue internationale de philosophie* 24 (1970) 321–337, especially 332–333.

164. Courcelle, *Recherches* 168–174.

165. *Art. cit.*

has well demonstrated, the eighth book is concerned with Augustine's liberation from the bonds of sexual concupiscence and again culminates in a reading from Paul. Furthermore, as I hope to show presently, this second reading is fictional and invented as a fitting climax to the eighth book, with its desperate struggle to break the bonds of sexual concupiscence.

So much then for the more obvious but unsuccessful method of searching Augustine's earlier works for descriptions to substantiate the details of the conversion-scene of the eighth book of the *Confessions.* A more scientific and much more successful technique consists of what may be termed "reference analysis." Thanks to his great love of the Scriptures, which he knew so thoroughly, Augustine's works are crowded with biblical references. It is my conviction that careful analysis of these references holds the possibility of divulging all kinds of interesting information.[166] In particular, and with reference to the present problem of the question of the authenticity of the well-known conversion-scene of the *Confessions*, such an approach holds the possibility of supplying persuasive evidence about Augustine's concern with the events of the conversion-scene in his earlier writings prior to the writing of the *Confessions.*

Thus, to take but one example for the present case, there is the interesting detail in the conversion-scene of the reading from Paul, which reading effects Augustine's con-

166. Thanks to The School of Computer Science of The University of New Brunswick which is presently hosting my 1981–82 sabbatical leave and to the assistance of Prof. Rodney H. Cooper, I am presently in the process of constructing a VSAM information-retrieval system for this very purpose.

version. According to *l'exactitude sténographique,* this is exactly what in fact occurred: after the momentous struggle against the bad habits of his past, Augustine was instantly converted by the reading of *Romans* 13, 13-14, in obedience to the mysterious voice, which he took to be of divine origin. However, granted this, and Augustine's immense memory, his passionate nature and his fondness for quoting from the Scriptures in general, and from Paul in particular, then it is well within the limits of human certainty that the impact of those verses from *Romans* will be found among the many scriptural references in his subsequent writing. In more concrete terms, if the detail of the miraculously directed reading is real fact, rather than artistic embellishment, then there must be enduring evidence of this factuality in his many references to *Romans* in his writings between the actual conversion in 386 and the description of it in the *Confessions* in 397-401.

According to my calculations,[167] Augustine's early writings up to, and including the *Confessions* contain about eight hundred and fifty verse-references[168] to *Romans* alone. As I have demonstrated elsewhere,[169]

167. These, and other such findings are based on the footnotes in the 1836-38 Gaume edition of the *Opera Omnia* of Augustine. Comparisons with certain works in the *Corpus Scriptorum Ecclesiasticorum Latinorum* have been most favourable. However a near-perfect system of establishing such references would involve computer comparisons of the text of Augustine's Bible with the latest critical editions of his works, something which, at least to my knowledge, has not yet been done.

168. Every verse is counted, every time there is a reference to it. Thus, *Romans* 13, 11-14 would count for four verse-references.

169. Leo C. Ferrari, 'Paul at the Conversion of Augustine; (Conf. VIII, 12, 29-30); *Augustinian Studies* 11 (1980) 5-20.

despite this plethora of references and Augustine's obvious preferences for quoting certain verses, not only is *Romans* 13, 13–14 not the subject anywhere of rapturous references, but it is not even to be found in the very earliest works, where it is most likely to occur. Nowhere, within the limits of my search, is there to be found the least spontaneous allusion to those verses which figure so prominently in the climax of the *Confessions*.

Furthermore, the *Exposition of Certain Propositions from the Epistle to the Romans* of 394 manages to all but ignore the verses in question. Only the last few words are selected for commentary and with such treatment that one can well wonder if the exegesis is indeed by the same person who underwent the soul-searing experience of the conversion-scene some mere eight years previously.[170]

It remains then, that *Romans* 13, 13–14 was *not* of particular interest to Augustine prior to the writing of the *Confessions,* nor, as far as I have been able to ascertain for at least some ten years thereafter.

It follows then, on the basis of all the evidence that I have been able to muster, that Augustine was not converted in the exact manner described in the *Confessions,* by the reading of *Romans* 13, 13–14, but rather that this detail is a dramatic embellishment invented by the gifted genius of Augustine. Further, its inspirational source seems to be the earlier passionate reading of Paul,[171] of which reading, the authenticity seems beyond doubt, if one is to be guided

170. *Op. cit.* 16–17.
171. *Conf.* 7, 21, 27.

by the additional allusions to it in *The Happy Life* and the *Answer to the Skeptics:* both of 386.

Again, while engaged in the previous research I was struck by the many similarities between Augustine's conversion and that of Paul. The falling to the ground, the affecting of the eyes and the hearing of a voice—these and other details suggested to me that the description of Augustine's conversion was indebted to that of Paul.[172] Perhaps most interesting of all, were certain uncanny similarities between the contents of the divine communications in both cases. Thus, each communication begins with a word which is repeated in the same discourse. Secondly, this word in one communication rhymes with the repeated word in the other communication. These features become obvious when one juxtaposes the two communications. On the one hand is Augustine's communication: *Tolle lege; tolle lege;* on the other hand is that of Paul: *Saule, Saule, quare me persequeris?* One is then confronted with the odd repetitiveness and rhyming in: *Tolle . . . tolle* and *Saule, Saule.*

The above various similarities suggest yet another and quite different approach to the question of the authenticity of the conversion-scene, but an approach which again uses the technique of reference analysis. This approach is based on the reasoning that if Augustine had been converted exactly as described in the details of the eighth book of the *Confessions,* then in the light of the above-mentioned similarities, he must certainly have been acutely aware of the close resemblance between his own conver-

172. *Acts* 9, 1–18; 22, 6–15; 26, 12–18.

sion and that of his beloved Paul. Again on the basis of reference analysis, one can expect to find evidence for, or against, the detailed factuality of the conversion-scene in the various writings of Augustine between the actual conversion in 386 and the description of it in the *Confessions* of 397–401.

In summary, this investigation resulted in findings in remarkable agreement with those of the previous one, but with some added important information.[173] Though references to Paul's conversion were found to be virtually absent from Augustine's early works, nevertheless, beginning in 396 and continuing through the very same years that he was working on the *Confessions,* there is to be found a most significant cluster of some fourteen references to that conversion of Paul. That makes a total of about fourteen references in a period of some six years. By comparison, in the twenty-eight years after the *Confessions,* from 402 to Augustine's death in 430, there are only some dozen references to Paul's conversion.

The conclusion is therefore that this study is doubly confirmative of the previous one. Not only is there an absence of allusions to Paul's conversion in the works prior to the writing of the *Confessions,* (thereby demonstrating that the conversion was not of particular significance to Augustine during that period), but there is also a most significant concentration of such allusions almost at the precise time that Augustine was working on that masterpiece.

173. See my 'Saint Augustine on the Road to Damascus,' *Augustinian Studies,* 13 (1982). The sermonal works constitute a class apart, and for reasons which are explained in my study.

Furthermore, the conclusion of this latter study is even more far-reaching than the previous one, which was concerned merely with the factuality of the reading from *Romans* 3, 13-14. This latter study concerns the factuality of the entire conversion-scene in the eighth book of the *Confessions*. From the evidence considered, it can only be concluded that this scene did not in fact transpire, but is rather both a fictional and a fitting climax to the fascinating story of the conversion of Augustine. On the other hand, it seems not entirely without foundation in the reality of his lived experience, in that the source of his inspiration for the scene seems to have been his earlier excited seizing upon the writings of Paul, and the subsequent passionate and prolonged reading of them. This occurred after the discovery of the so-called "books of the Platonists" and is an event of which the factuality cannot be doubted, due to its corroboration in several works of Augustine, as has been seen.

Before concluding this section on the description of Augustine's conversion, as set out in the *Confessions,* it is also noteworthy that Augustine's reception into the Church was probably not as straightforward as the narrative would suggest. Like his beloved Paul before him, he was probably regarded as a notorious character by the Christian community. Thus, as he himself informs us, among the things that confirmed him in his error as a Manichee were his many victories in debates against Christians.[174] If his victories were anything like those of his

174. *On Two Souls, against the Manichaeans* 11 & 12; *Conf.* 3, 12, 21.

68

debates after his conversion, then in the eyes of the Christian community, he must have been a very notorious character indeed. It would follow therefore, that his professed desire to be received into the Church must have been greeted with great circumspection and perhaps even incredulity. Such a conclusion certainly seems to be borne out by the way that Ambrose repeatedly ignored him.[175] The result of this silent snubbing seems to have been that it was to Simplicianus, the "spiritual father" of Ambrose that the inquiring Augustine went, in order to find out how he might set his feet upon the pathway that leads to eternal salvation.[176]

Courcelle has presented convincing evidence that the importance of this encounter with Simplicianus has been greatly underrated. For one thing, it seems that there was not one meeting, as the text of the *Confessions* seems to imply, but rather a whole series.[177] Furthermore, Simplicianus was not only the spiritual father of Ambrose (with all that that implied), but also the leading figure at Milan in a daring attempt to christianize Neoplatonism; a fact which prompts Courcelle to conclude that not only did Augustine consult the holy Simplicianus about his spiritual disarray, but also went to him for information about a christianized Neoplatonism.[178] Such a purpose would have been in keeping with the persistent desire of Augustine which, as we have seen, was to find a philosophy

175. *Conf.* 6, 3, 3. See also the article of footnote 140.
176. *Conf.* 8, 1, 1; 8, 2, 3.
177. *Recherches* pp. 168–174.
178. *Recherches* p. 171.

which incorporated the name of Christ. In this perspective, a series of visits with Simplicianus, thereby gives him a vital role in Augustine's quest for *philosophia;* a search which was completed in one respect by his reception into the Church. However, as will be seen, the role of Simplicianus also becomes vital at another less recognized conversion of the inquiring Augustine.

(ii)   The Final Conversion

Anton Pegis, in an article entitled "The Second Conversion of St. Augustine," [179] has ventured to identify this conversion with the growth since his baptism as indicated by the tenth book of the *Confessions*. [180] It seems to me that there is indeed all this and more. I hope to explain that there is much more involved than merely a quantitative growth in Augustine's spirituality. A profound qualitative transformation occurs, inasmuch as there is not merely a building upon the foundations already laid, but a momentous change to new foundations. In short, it is what I would call a tremendous transformation. It seems to me that the resulting radical change in religious belief rightly deserves the title of conversion.

As was said at the conclusion of the chapter on Augustine's conversion to *philosophia*, with the discovery of Neoplatonism he had at last reached the long-sought port of philosophy. The sea-voyage was over. However, his

179. Pp. 79–93 in *Gesellschaft, Kultur, Literarur; Rezeption und Originilität im Wachsen einer europäischen Literatur und Geistkeit.* Beiträge Liutpold Wallach gewidmet. Stuttgart, 1975.

180. *Art. cit.* p. 84.

journey was just beginning. Before him lay the hinterland where he was eventually to come down to earth in more ways than one, but still without losing sight of his heavenly goal.

For one thing, Augustine's enforced ordination as presbyter in 391 meant a complete change in the conditions of his life. Previously, having rejected his worldly profession of orator, he was living in retirement, surrounded by his friends, and engaged in the leisurely pursuit of philosophy. His ordination in 391 abruptly changed all that. He was thrust back into the public eye and, as shepherd to his flock, became the confidant of every man. Furthermore, just as there was to be no more leisure time for the pursuit of philosophy, so too his new duties required that the whole focus of his intense mind now shift permanently in what may be termed a Plotinian manner, from the many to the one: from the many books of the philosophers to the one Book whose author was God. So, the Holy Scriptures whose simple style had once repelled his erudite inquiries now became the exclusive domain of his ongoing investigations.

As we know from Augustine's writings, the principal guide in that inquiry was the apostle Paul, whose books now claimed Augustine's closest attention. Despite the impression given by the *Confessions*,[181] this was not his first encounter with Paul's writings. During his nine years or so as a Manichee, Augustine would have become quite conversant with Paul's writings, at least in an expurgated

181. See my article: 'Augustine's Discovery of Paul,' *Augustinian Studies,* (in press).

71

form.[182] Indeed, as has been observed by Ries, Paul had become quite a favourite of the Manichees.[183] Considering also the authority of Paul, both in the Scriptures and also in Augustine's environment of the time,[184] Augustine's important preoccupation now was to define himself in terms of his own interpretation of Paul over and against that of the Manichees.[185] As considerations will show, this resulted in a fundamental shift in Augustine's perspective; a shift resulting in what I shall call his "final conversion."

In order to appreciate the aspect of that shift which is germane to present considerations, it is important to recall a fundamental assumption which had permeated Augustine's earlier writings, and indeed is responsible for a large measure of their subject matter. This is the conviction (deriving from the newly-discovered Neoplatonism) that it was possible, even in the present life, and by means of one's own efforts, to rise to a sustained intellectual communion with the divine reality. Van Fleteren has given us an extensive and lucid exposition of the importance of this motive in Augustine's earliest works and its relation to the well-known ascent of the soul in the seventh book of the *Confessions*.[186] Besides moral and mental purification,

182. Julian Ries, 'La Bible chez saint Augustin et chez les Manichéens,' *Revue des Etudes Augustiniennes* 7 (1961) 231–243; 9 (1963) 201–215; 10 (1964) 309–329.

183. *Art. cit.* 10 (1964) 323.

184. Brown, p. 151ff.

185. Brown, p. 153.

186. F. E. Van Fleteren, OSA, 'Augustine's Ascent of the Soul in Book VII of the Confessions; A Reconsideration,' *Augustinian Studies* 5 (1974) 29–72; as also his 'The Early Works of Augustine and his Ascent at Milan,' *Studies in Medieval Culture* 10 (1977) 19–23.

the venture also involved the liberal arts as the means *par excellence* of attaining union with the divine. Thus, as Augustine himself informs us, this was the principal motive behind the series of textbooks which he planned and only partially wrote.[187] Even so, the fundamental idea so permeates Augustine's earlier writings that Brown has fittingly remarked that those works are essentially programmes for perfection.[188]

Nevertheless, within a decade, by the time he came to writing the *Confessions*, all that early exuberance, together with the confidence which had sustained and nourished it, had vanished. Something drastic had happened.

Among other things, the new life forced upon him by his ordination was not without effect also upon his former ideals. As a result, there now remained time neither for leisure nor for the pursuit of philosophy. Moreover, by virtue of his ecclesiastical duties, he had been thrust rudely back into the world which he had so strongly rejected. The effect upon Augustine must have been very disconcerting indeed. So drastic was the change that Brown considers that by the time of the *Confessions*, he had become a man with a lost future:

> If Augustine could not take his friends for granted any longer, still less could he understand himself in terms of his old ideals. We met him at Cassiciacum, as a man certain of his future: his books are all of them programmes; even his reminiscences are no more than a list of those obstacles to perfection, which he hoped soon to

187. *Retractions* 1, 6.
188. Brown, p. 156.

73

> surmount. In the *Confessions* he is a man who has lost this certain future . . . he is obsessed by the need to understand what had really happened to him in his distant past.[189]

Until very recently I had agreed with that verdict. However, in the long labour of preparing this lecture, I have come to the very opposite conclusion. By the time of coming to writing the *Confessions*. Augustine had become a man uncannily certain of his future, but it was no longer the future of his earlier writings. For one thing, he now regarded those writings as written in God's service indeed, but as principally breathing the pride of the schools.[190]

As I shall explain, the reason for the changed perspective was not merely that Augustine's manifold ecclesiastical duties had left him no leisure for the pursuit of philosophy and interest in it had disappeared simply because of neglect. I suggest that the ultimate explanation for the changed perspective lies in what I have termed Augustine's final conversion.

The principal source of this change seems to lie in Augustine's intense ongoing study of Paul. In 1974, Alflatt (then a graduate student of mine, I am proud to say) published a fine study which located the precise beginning of Augustine's revolutionary change in perspective.[191] According to that study, the change ultimately stems from the debate with the Manichee, Fortunatus, on the 28th and 29th of August, 392, of which Alflatt observes in a subsequent study:

189. Brown, p. 156.

190. *Conf.* 9, 4, 7; *On Christian Doctrine* 2, 13, 20; 4, 7, 14.

191. Malcolm E. Alflatt, 'The Development of the Idea of Involuntary Sin in St. Augustine,' *Revue des Etudes Augustiniennes* 20 (1974) 113–134.

> In that debate Augustine had been compelled to admit
> for the first time, under the persuasion of certain
> Pauline texts ably wielded by Fortunatus, that men do
> sin of necessity. That admission contains the germ of all
> Augustine's later understanding of man's helplessness,
> an understanding which contrasted so starkly with the
> view held in his earlier works, that man was capable of
> doing good and avoiding evil by virtue of his free will.[192]

We have then, in that epochal encounter of 392, the
beginnings of a change which was to gather momentum in
the immediately following years, as Augustine became in-
creasingly immersed in the now urgent study of Paul. In
summary, the change in his perspective involved an ever-
increasing minimization of the role of man's free will in his
own salvation, and in a complementary fashion, the growing importance of divine omnipotence. By the same
token, Augustine the philosopher of human freedom was
being transformed into Augustine the theologian of the
omnipotent divine will, and in the process, the entire foundations of Augustine's thought were shifting. So began
the process of the final conversion.

By means of one of those coincidences which seemed
too apposite to be imputed entirely to the realm of mere
chance, the climax to this profound change came in the
year 396. It was then that Augustine received a letter from
Simplicianus, asking his interpretation of certain difficult
passages of Scripture.[193] This was the very same Simpli-

192. Malcolm E. Alflatt, 'The Responsibility for Involuntary Sin in
Saint Augustine,' *Recherches Augustiniennes* 10 (1975) 171-186. The
quote is on p. 171. See also: Malcolm E. Alflatt, *The Ontological
Grounding of Moral Responsibility in the Thought of St. Augustine,* MA
Thesis, The University of New Brunswick, 1974, 137 pp.

193. *Letter 37.*

cianus to whom, just ten years earlier, Augustine had gone to inquire about the best means of putting his foot on the way that led to salvation.[194] Of particular relevance to the present topic is the fact that one of Simplicianus' passages was *Romans* 9, 10-29, where Paul was discussing the rejection of Esau by God and the election of Jacob.

It was in response to the problems that he saw posed by this enigma that Augustine now produced an answer in complete opposition to anything that he had previously held. However, as Babcock has convincingly shown, it was an answer towards which he had been slowly but surely pushed during the few preceding years of poring over the works of Paul.[195] Despite those years of evolution, Augustine was acutely aware of the momentous change which was now occurring as he wrestled with the problem of the election of Jacob and the rejection of Esau. In fact, some thirty years later, when mentioning the transformation, he likened it to a battle of the human will against the grace of God.[196]

In his new perspective, he came to see salvation as the consequence of an unfathomable choice by God, made regardless of personal merits. As a result, salvation came *entirely* from God, without the faintest traces of human merit, whether actual or potential. At last he came to see the full truth of the words of *I Corinthians* 4, 7: "What do

194. *Conf.* 8, 1, 1; 8, 2, 3.

195. William S. Babcock, 'Augustine's Interpretation of Romans (A.D. 394–396),' *Augustinian Studies* 10 (1979) 55–74. See especially pp. 65–67.

196. *On the Predestination of the Saints* 4, 8; *Cf. Retractions* 2, 1, 1.

you have that you did not receive?"[197] Such, in essence, was the substance of Augustine's reply to Simplicianus.[198] It followed too, in keeping with Paul's example, that man was related to God as the clay to the potter, to be shaped for better or for worse, according as the potter saw fit.[199]

Obviously, the shift in perspective was no mere quantitative one. As was said earlier, it was a tremendous transformation in the very foundations of Augustine's thought. Furthermore, it was no conclusion reached on the basis of mere human reasoning. Indeed, as Augustine tells us, it was a veritable revelation to him from God Himself, as he struggled to answer the question of Simplicianus—"This, God revealed to me as I sought to solve this question when I was writing, as I said, to the Bishop Simplicianus."[200] Consequently, Augustine's perspective was profoundly and permanently changed, as he himself well realized.[201] This transformation is what I mean by the final conversion of Saint Augustine.

I mentioned before that Augustine's early quest for *philosophia* disappeared after his ordination, due both to lack of leisure and also to excess of ecclesiastical duties. As

197. *Retractions* 2, 1, 1.

198. *To Simplicianus; On Various Questions* 1, q. 2, on *Romans* 9, 10–29.

199. *Romans* 9, 20–21. *Cf. Isaiah* 29, 16; 45, 9.

200. *On the Predestination of the Saints* 4, 8. (Holmes & Wallis translation). I am sure that Augustine would be the very first to disagree with Brown's comparison of his revelation to the experiences of a modern speculative thinker. (Brown, p. 280, n. 2). See also A. C. de Veer, 'Revelare, Revalatio; Eléments d'une étude sur l'emploi du mot et sur la signification chez S. Augustin,' *Recherches Augustiniennes* 2 (1962) 331–357, especially 352–354.

201. *On the Predestination of the Saints* 2, 3 onwards.

if these factors were not enough, there was now the added influence of the changed perspective arising from his final conversion. It seems to me that this new perspective would have rendered quite obvious to Augustine the basic flaw in the whole project of the earlier quest for *philosophia*. That flaw was the proud assumption that by dint of self-discipline and self-purification it was possible to elevate oneself to an enduring vision of the divine essence, even in the present life. Such an assumption was now obviously incompatible with the new revelation that *everything*, from the very first stirrings of grace onwards, came not from man (as Augustine had previously assumed), but from God and from God alone. *I Corinthians* 4, 7 now became an absolute truth: "What do you have that you did not receive?"

Masterful strategist that he was, Augustine could not but have been acutely conscious of the manifold challenges that would face him as a result of his final conversion. In this regard, Brown, with his usual perceptiveness, has remarked that Augustine's reply to Simplicianus on the problems posed by *Romans* 9, 10–29, was really the charter for the *Confessions*.[202] When one considers the unifying implication of divine election which constitutes the very substance of the book, there is certainly much to warrant Brown's opinion. In addition, there is the added dimension that the subject of that divine predilection was Augustine himself.

The more immediate grounds for such a conclusion were the events which had transpired since his conversion

202. Brown, p. 170.

to the Catholic Church in 386. His enforced ordination in 391 was followed in the next year by the triumphant debate against his former friend, Fortunatus the Manichee. In 393, though a mere presbyter, Augustine addressed the General Council of the Bishops of Africa, then meeting in Hippo. In 395 he was appointed successor to Bishop Valerius of the same town, assuming the full responsibility of the position in the succeeding year, with the death of the aged Valerius. One of the first things which Augustine did after his consecration as Bishop of Hippo Regius was to undertake his reply to the letter of Simplicianus; an arduous task indeed, as has been noted. But it was also a holy labour bringing with it the God-given revelation which was to transform Augustine's perspective for ever afterwards. And so occurred the final conversion.

Important as these recent events were, none of them found their way into the narrative of the *Confessions*. They may well have been the signs of divine predilection, but the real roots of Augustine's convictions in this regard lay further back in his past. The episodes most illustrative of that predilection are recorded indelibly in the pages of his *Confessions*. There, as the title indicates,[203] Augustine confesses before God and before man, the glory and the mercy of God as vividly illustrated by the events of Augustine's own sinful past.

Today, in surveying the pages of the *Confessions*, one is struck by the same leitmotif of the entire work: despite his rebellious sinfulness and his most obstinate resistance

203. J. Ratzinger, 'Originalität und Überlieferung in Augustins Begriff der Confessio,' *Revue des Etudes Augustiniennes* 3 (1957) 375–392.

to divine grace, God draws Augustine inexorably towards Himself. Such, in essence, was the way Augustine surveyed his past life. The conclusion was inescapable: through no fault, or merit of his own, Augustine was the subject of divine predilection.

However, for Augustine at the time, this was merely one instance of a far more important general revelation which had been granted him. It was too, a revelation which at all costs must rise above the impending challenges of human error.

It is important to realize that the masterwork of the *Confessions* was composed in the wake of Augustine's final conversion, with all that that implied. As I see it, the prime purpose of the work was the purposeful rebuttal of all the anticipated violent reactions which were sure to be aroused by the revelation granted him of a divine predilection, or rejection, which operated entirely independently of human merits, or sinfulness.

As the perceptive Pincherle has explained, the transformed perspective of Augustine, contained in his reply to Simplicianus, sent shock waves through the Christian world of his time,[204] alienating him even from close friends and making him doubly hateful to old enemies. It also gained him some new ones. Among the representatives of Christian consternation was the Englishman, Pelagius, destined to begin the Pelagian controversy,[205] which was to claim a considerable portion of Augustine's attention for

204. Alberto Pincherle, 'Intorno alla genesi delle Confessioni di S. Agostini,' *Augustinian Studies* 5 (1974) 167-176.

205. G.Martinetto, 'Les premières réactions antiaugustiniennes de Pélage,' *Revue des Etudes Augustiniennes* 17 (1971) 83-117.

the rest of his days. In the course of this controversy he elaborated the theory of predestination for which he later became famous.[206] As to the impending controversy itself, Augustine had anticipated the events, in a very general way, some years before they were upon him.

Just how realistic were his anticipations, was subsequently demonstrated by the protracted polemics of the Pelagians. But, masterful strategist that he was, Augustine was well prepared for their worst assaults upon his position which he now held by God's revelation. Indeed, he anticipated their attacks so well, that as he himself said towards the end of his life, he was cutting down a future Pelagian heresy even before it appeared on the scene. Accordingly, in his *On the Gift of Perserverance*, written as late as 428/9, he observes about his writings and the Pelagians:

> Those very treatises of mine were both composed and published before the Pelagians had begun to appear; and they do not see in how many passages of those treatises I was unawares cutting down a future Pelagian heresy, by preaching the grace by which God delivers us from evil errors and from our habits, without any preceding merit of ours,—doing this according to His gratuitous mercy. And this I began more fully to apprehend in that disputation which I wrote to Simplicianus the Bishop of the Church of Milan, of blessed memory, in the beginning of my episcopate, when, moreover, I both perceived and asserted that the beginning of faith is God's gift.[207]

206. H. Rondet, SJ, 'La prédestination augustinienne; genèse d'une doctrine,' *Science Ecclésiastiques* 18 (1966) 229–261.

207. *Op. cit* 20, 52.

81

It is my opinion that the story of the *Confessions* is the vivid and masterly portrayal of just such a transformation, recounting Augustine's deliverance from errors and bad habits without any preceding merits on his part, and indeed the story of a transformation for the purpose already intimated. By telling it Augustine was already anticipating the very worst attacks upon his new position. Furthermore, by throwing his past sinful life open to public scrutiny he was also disarming his enemies ahead of time by depriving them of the deadly weapons of slander. As a result, his position therefore became quite unassailable. Also, by recounting his sinful past and his subsequent redemption, not because of the slightest merit on his part, but solely as living proof of God's gratuitous mercy, then his principal argument of the *Confessions* became impregnable. The tactical genius of Augustine therefore won out on both fronts.

Considering the strategic importance of the *Confessions*, it is understandable that Augustine expended much time and care upon its composition, besides bringing every resource of his not inconsiderable education and this towering genius to bear upon the task. According to modern calculations, it occupied him for some five years from 397 to 401.[208] Also, as has been seen, during this same time-period, he acquired his first protracted interest in the conversion of Paul. The labours were rewarded, as the work became a very popular classic, even during his own life-time.[209] Subsequently, for nigh on sixteen cen-

208. A. Solignac, pp. 45–54 in *Les Confessions I–VII,* (vol. 13 in *Oeuvres de saint Augustin,* Bibliothèque Augustinienne, Paris, 1962).

209. *Retractions* 2, 6, 1.

turies, the *Confessions* has stood the test of time, standing like a mighty fortress guarding the branch in the path which Augustine's thought followed after his final conversion. Understandably then, towards the end of his life, when addressing a treatise to two of his friends, he observed of the *Confessions* in regard to the Pelagians:

> In those same books of the *Confessions*, in respect of what I have already related concerning my conversion, when God converted me to that faith which, with a most miserable and raging talkativeness, I was destroying, do you not remember that it was so narrated how I showed that it was granted to the faithful and daily tears of my mother, that I should not perish?[210]

Here, in the mention of his tearful mother, Monica, who prayed daily for the return of her son to the Catholic Faith of his childhood, we have the very source of all Augustine's certitude. She it was, to whom he imputed the cause of everything that he lived.[211] Elsewhere in his early works she is depicted as the voice for a wisdom whose source is divine.[212] It is in this last-mentioned role that Monica is featured throughout the *Confessions*.[213]

Great as was Augustine's appreciation of his mother's virtues in his earlier works, by the time that he came to writing the *Confessions* there was an added dimension to the immensity of his indebtedness to her. As the pages of that masterpiece testify, she had followed him relentlessly

210. *On the Gift of Perseverance* 20, 53.

211. *The Happy Life* 6: "mater nostra, cujus meriti credo esse omne quod vivo."

212. *The Happy Life* 2, 10.

213. Leo C. Ferrari, 'The Dreams of Monica in Augustine's Confessions,' *Augustinian Studies* 10 (1979) 3–17.

in his defiant flight across the sea. But, as subsequent events proved, it was an action for which she was to pay the supreme earthly price. Moreover, by a bitter twist of circumstances, Augustine found himself implicated in her death.[214]

Fittingly therefore, the latter half of the ninth, and last autobiographical book of the *Confessions* closes with a lengthy eulogy of the mother who had laid down her life for the conversion of her wayward son. It seems to me also, that it is no mere coincidence that the writing of that masterpiece began on the tenth anniversary of her death.

In conclusion then, we have followed saint Augustine through the successive stages of his various conversions which were ultimately constitutive of the final personality of the great Bishop of Hippo Regius. Since he is also the principal founding Father of Western Christianity, we cannot know too much about him. In regard to such knowledge, as we have seen, his many surviving works offer precious insights into the pages of the *Confessions*. May these exemplary insights bring us to live to the end of our lives the concluding prayer of the *Confessions: A te petatur, in te quaeratur, ad te pulsetur: sic, sic accipietur, sic invenietur, sic aperietur*—"Let it be asked of Thee, sought in Thee, knocked for at Thee: so, even so shall it be received, so shall it be found, so shall it be opened."— *Amen.*

214. See my 'The Background to Augustine's City of God,' *The Classical Journal* (U.S.A.) 67 (1972) 198–208, especially 204–205.

THE SAINT AUGUSTINE LECTURES

1959 *Saint Augustine on Personality,* by Paul Henry, S.J., Institut Catholique, Paris; New York, The Macmillan Company, 1960.

1960 *Platonism and Augustinianism,* by Raymond Klibansky, McGill University; unpublished.

1961 *Charter of Christendom: the Significance of the City of God,* by John O'Meara, University College, Dublin; New York, The Macmillan Company, 1961.

1962 *At the Origins of the Thomistic Notion of Man,* by Anton Pegis, Pontifical Institute of Mediaeval Studies, Toronto; New York, The Macmillan Company, 1963.

1963 *Augustine's View of Reality,* by Vernon J. Bourke, St. Louis University; Villanova, Villanova Press, 1964.

1964 *Augustine and the Greek Philosophers,* by John F. Callahan, Georgetown University; Villanova, Villanova University Press, 1967.

1965   *The Resurrection and Saint Augustine's Theology of Human Values,* by Henri I. Marrou, University of Paris; Villanova University Press, 1966.

1966   *St. Augustine and Christian Platonism,* by A. Hilary Armstrong, University of Liverpool; Villanova, Villanova University Press, 1967.

1967   *Saint Augustine on Creation,* by Paul Henry, S.J., Institut Catholique, Paris; University of California, San Diego; unpublished.

1968   *Augustine on Immortality,* by John A. Mourant, The Pennsylvania State University, University Park, Pa.; Villanova, Villanova University Press, 1969.

1969   *Augustinian Personalism,* by Mary T. Clark, R.S.C.J., Manhattanville College, Post-Doctoral Fellow, Yale University; Villanova, Villanova University Press, 1970.

1970   *Augustine and Modern Research on Pelagianism,* by Gerald Bonner, Durham University, England; Villanova, Villanova University Press, 1972.

1971   *Political Idealism and Christianity in the Thought of St. Augustine,* by Ernest L. Fortin, Boston College; Villanova, Villanova University Press, 1972.

1972   *Saint Augustin et la dialectique,* by Jean Pépin. École Pratique des Hautes Études, Paris; Villanova, Villanova University Press, 1976.

1973   *Augustine's Strategy as an Apologist,* by Eugene TeSelle, Vanderbilt University, Nashville, Tennessee; Villanova, Villanova University Press, 1974.

1974   *Church, State and Toleration: An Intriguing Change of Mind in Augustine,* by Emilien Lamirande, University of Ottawa, Ottawa, Canada; Villanova, Villanova University Press, 1975.

1975   *St. Augustine's Monasticism in the Light of Acts 4.32–35,* by Luc Verheijen, O.S.A., École Pratique des Hautes Études, Paris; Villanova, Villanova University Press, 1979.

1976   *The Confessions of St. Augustine: A Reappraisal,* by Alberto Pincherle, Professor Emeritus, University of Rome, printed in Volume 7, *Augustinian Studies;* Villanova, Augustinian Institute, 1976.

1977   *The Creation of Man in St. Augustine's De Genesi ad Litteram,* by John J. O'Meara, University College, Dublin; Villanova, Villanova University Press, in press.

1978   *Joy in Augustine's Ethics,* by Vernon J. Bourke, Professor Emeritus, St. Louis University; Villanova, Villanova University Press, 1979.

1979   *Saint Augustine on Memory,* by John A. Mourant, Professor Emeritus, The Pennsylvania State University, University Park, Pa.; Villanova, Villanova University Press, 1980.

1980   *Regio Beatitudinis. Augustine's Concept of Happiness,* by Werner Beierwaltes, Albert Ludwigs Universität, Freiburg; Villanova, Villanova University Press, 1981.

1981   *Saint Augustine's Platonism,* by Robert J. O'Connell, S.J., Fordham University; Villanova, Villanova University Press, 1984.

Publications of:

AUGUSTINIAN INSTITUTE

Villanova University
Villanova, PA 19085

the field of Augustinian studies. The first product of this venture will be a team-developed Concordance to the *Confessions* of Saint Augustine. He is also the author of a forthcoming book on computer programming.

• • • •

With its rare combination of penetrating insights and meticulous scientific analysis, this revolutionary study provides completely new interpretations of the religious development of Saint Augustine. By combining textual evidence from Augustine's writings with certain precisely dated spectacles of astronomy, the author argues cogently for the perceptible influence of those celestial phenomena upon Augustine's early conversion to Manicheism, as well as his later disillusionment with it. Also, on the basis of a careful analysis of Augustine's many scriptural references, the famous conversion-scene of the *Confessions* is shown to be modeled upon the conversion of Saint Paul. Finally, the author argues that the *Confessions* itself is a most powerful testament to Augustine's final conversion to a completely arbitrary form of divine predestinarianism.